'A brilliantly creative way to explore _____ that emerge from a classic fil_____ is heartwarming, winsom_____ nd enjoy a delightful jou_____
Jeff Lucas, author, speake.

'Bryony writes with hum_____ ⁀ as insight. You'll never be able to wa_____ ᵤᵤns in quite the same way.'
Rev Canon Kate Bottley, broadcaster and Anglican priest

'Bryony's inspiring work on this much-loved musical draws out beautiful insights into the many and varied themes contained in the von Trapp story. Anyone viewing the film after reading this book will find they won't just be watching a movie, but will be embarking on an adventure with God!'
Rev Canon Michael Mitton, writer, spiritual director, speaker

'I have many happy memories of watching *The Sound of Music* with my children – it became the soundtrack to several family holidays. So I encouraged Bryony to write her own "musings" as a fun way of helping others reflect on life, faith and their "favourite things". Bryony has a beautiful style of writing which will help anyone find God in the ordinary.'
Martyn Snow, Bishop of Leicester; Chair of the Archbishops' Council for Evangelists

'In this joy-filled book, Bryony takes a familiar musical film and shows us how it speaks of God. Storylines and songs alike become windows to a deeper dimension, carefully crafted and beautifully written. A book to inspire and uplift; read it for yourself and buy it as a gift for someone special.'
Tony Horsfall, author and retreat leader

'Hooray! A devotional book which has as much fun and joy as it does depth. This is wonderfully inventive writing, a celebration of creativity and a rare affirmation of media and the arts. I dare you to read it and not want to climb trees while dressed in curtains.'
Frances Finn, broadcaster and Church of England priest

'Bryony writes in such a lovely and inspirational style to share gospel truths in a fun but thought-provoking way. An enjoyable read, this book of "musings" is easy to dip in and out of as each short chapter draws you into a scene, then leaves you pondering…'
Judith Mayho, Registered Nurse and part of the leadership team at Tunbridge Wells Christian Centre

'Bryony takes a unique approach to a film that means such a lot to so many people. Through sensitive engagement with the depth and detail of the story, Bryony draws out many parallels to the Christian life today, covering a wide range of topics such as conflict, play and care for the environment. Helpful, gentle questions and a prayer are set out at the end of each section to encourage thoughtful engagement with the story, often with practical exercises to aid reflection. This is a lovely book for anyone who has fond memories of the film, or even those coming to it for the first time.'
Rev Dr Jenny Corcoran, Tutor for Lay Education, Practical Theology and Old Testament, St Augustine's College of Theology

Dear Lin.
With love.

Bryony Wood x

The Sound of Musings

"Climb Every Mountain
till you find your dream"
x.

Bryony Wood

instant
apostle

First published in Great Britain in 2023

Instant Apostle
104A The Drive
Rickmansworth
Herts
WD3 4DU

Many thanks to Debbie Cortese and Chris Hodgson at Core Publications Ltd for the original cover inspiration/design and promotional images.

British Library Cataloguing-in-Publication Data

A catalogue record for this book is available from the British Library.

This book and all other Instant Apostle books are available from Instant Apostle:

Website: www.instantapostle.com

Email: info@instantapostle.com

ISBN 978-1-912726-71-4

Printed in Great Britain.

Dedication

For Carl:
for without you I'd be a dried-up prune;
a dehydrated husk of shrivelled humanity in
a chair-shaped slump in front of a blank computer.
Thank you for your encouragement, unconditional love
and your endless supply of coffee, tea and sandwiches.
For your patience when I'd 'nip upstairs to finish a
paragraph' and emerge five hours later...
Thank you for reading and editing my many typos
and making my ramblings more 'sensical';
even when I made up new words that you'd laugh at.
Thank you for giving me edelweiss.
Thank you for bringing our home alive with the sound of
music.
You are my 'Captain' and my 'Mother Abbess' rolled into
one.

Contents

Introduction

Since 1965, the Hollywood blockbuster *The Sound of Music* has, rather like Marmite or peanut butter, divided people into two camps: those who love it and those who don't. For those who love it, the story and its songs have provided a soundtrack of joy for decades and still offers a feel-good factor today.

I remember the first time I watched Maria singing and swirling atop that iconic mountain as the film began. I was utterly transfixed, for it was my first experience of proper cinema, wedged between my mum, aunty and grandma. My generation, the post-baby boomers, then had to wait a *very* long time for it to be shown on television (Christmas Day 1978). Then another wait for the video, and later the DVD, copies to be released – only then could I watch it on demand and introduce it to the next generation, or two.

Today I still watch it with a smile and a song, albeit a very quiet song, because someone in the house will be moaning, 'You're not watching that film again'! So, quite simply, there are, I suggest, few films that have stayed as fresh and wholesome as this one.

The sincerest form of flattery is, they say, to be mimicked, imitated or reproduced, so it's not surprising that parodies and reminders of *The Sound of Music* frequently circulate on social media. It has become part of our national shared soundtrack. The title song 'The Hills

11

are Alive' was chosen in the UK's Covid lockdown edition of BBC's *Desert Island Discs* in 2020, and 'Climb Every Mountain' was one of the showstoppers included in the 2022 concert for the Queen's Platinum Jubilee. While visiting London recently, I heard one busker playing 'Edelweiss', and another further along sang 'My Favorite Things'. Proof, if proof is needed, how so many *Sound of Music* songs are indeed part of our national consciousness.

Even American presidents choose to listen to *The Sound of Music*. When listening recently to a recording of Barak Obama reading from his book *A Promised Land*,[1] I was heartened to learn that he would listen to particular songs before a big debate, including John Coltrane's version of 'My Favorite Things'. And because the film is based on historical events and set in a real place, visitors still flock to Salzburg to visit *Sound of Music* locations, thereby keeping alive the songs and story.

So it seems that almost everyone knows about the nun who ran across the hills and became a governess to the von Trapp children. Few of us would fail to recognise the scene of Maria and the children running across the meadows dressed in their refashioned, upscaled curtains, or the prompt to start at the (very) beginning…

Woven throughout the script and songs are subtle prompts that speak of faith. It is not a 'Christian' film, or a film with an agenda to proselytise. Yet should we choose to, we can be inspired by Maria's journey and explore what it is to live life in all its fullness and trust God. My prayer is that, like Maria, we too can all discover God's will for our life.

---

[1] Barack Obama, *A Promised Land* (NY: Viking, 2020).

Everything I have written is borne out of respect for the show, its characters and songs. I am aware that, whether on stage or screen, it's a dramatic interpretation of a real family. And although the historical Maria and her captain are now deceased, there are members of the extended von Trapp family who are still very much alive. Their real story didn't necessarily match the musical interpretation, yet that's the interpretation we have become familiar with and the inspiration for these musings. My hope is that any members of the von Trapp family can be assured that *The Sound of Musings* seeks to honour the legacy of *The Sound of Music* as the film celebrates its sixtieth anniversary in 2025. And if Julie Andrews ever does read this, then I'd love you to know that you truly, utterly nailed Maria's role!

If you have watched this film before, you may enjoy another viewing before or while reading this book; and if you're a newbie to *The Sound of Music*, then why not see what all the fuss is about and watch it! For although I explain each scene as we go along, it may make more sense if you've seen the movie; it will also give a context for each chapter.

I'd also suggest this is a book to muse over, to take your time reading and reflecting upon each chapter; but it is your book now, so up to you! However, wherever and whenever you read it – may you too, like Maria, discover the joy and depth of God's love as you discern His will for your life.

I now invite you to join me and follow Maria's story from the opening scene and discover something different about this iconic divine and human love story.

Bryony Wood

1
The Hills Are Alive

It is almost impossible to actually say those words without the inflection of the melody, so used are we to the majestic overture to one of the most popular films ever made. As the opening credits of the film unfold, the camera soars over beautiful Austrian mountains and valleys before swooping down over villages and meadows.

Like every compelling story, this one is about people; one particular nun and a wealthy but emotionally struggling family. Like every single human story, it has a framework – a space and place that holds the unfolding narrative. The opening credits give us a stunning backdrop, a context for the story that is about to be told.

Those initial sweeping aerial views give us opportunity to marvel at the beauty of hills that are literally alive with the sound of music. Now, as then, cowbells jingle as birds sing and the breeze whispers through trees, while, brooks trickle and splash through flower-filled meadows. All of nature's sounds, the natural music of creation to reflect and praise the Creator.

The scenery is a major attraction of this film, but also it is an invitation to appreciate God's incredible handiwork. The geology and ecology, the natural and the humanly shaped world offer evidence that not just Maria, but we too are players in a bigger story.

Beyond this film, there is a book of the 'big story' that we are invited to read. It starts with the opening lines of Genesis, revealing God as producer and director, the source of life Himself. In those first verses of the Bible, before even time itself begins, God – Father, Son, and Holy Spirit – snaps the celestial clapboard and rolls the angelic cameras to create and reveal His eternal blockbuster. He speaks His first line of public dialogue and life and light erupt into being. Then, at the climax of that opening scene, humanity is created to become the pinnacle, the most cherished part of creation: 'It is very good,'[2] God says with great satisfaction.

All of us, without exception, are invited through the beauty of creation to marvel at something so incredible yet utterly commonplace, so familiar yet so finely tuned. Into this awe-inspiring wonder, God offers us a playground and workplace, a resting place and life-source so that we can feast upon it to feed our souls and bodies.

However, if we just gaze at creation as an object, then we miss the greatest gift of all. For there is hollow joy in beauty if we merely watch creation without engaging with the author of creation Himself. What we see all around us offers evidence of intelligent creation and a creator offering an invitation to respond, as the apostle Paul wrote in his letter to the Romans:

> For what can be known about God is plain to them, because God has shown it to them. Ever since the

---

[2] See Genesis 1:31.

creation of the world his eternal power and divine nature, invisible though they are, have been understood and seen through the things he has made.

(Romans 1:19-20)

Each sunset, each bird that rises from lake to tree, each raindrop on each rose; each different landscape points us to the Holy One who spoke all of this into being. This is no hidden drama, no secret plan; the evidence for and of a creator is offered by every atom of creation itself. All is created by Him for us to relish, to tend and to enjoy; all designed to perfection with supreme artistry and unconditional love; all designed to point us towards the very source of life and love Himself.

Moments for musing

Where do you notice creation bursting with life around you?

How might you develop more of a holy habit of intentionally looking at God's creation? What might you do to turn that into praise and prayer?

How could you reflect something of God's creativity by developing your own creativity? It doesn't need to be 'perfect'; just creating something new can be surprisingly restorative.

Prayer

*Dear Lord, open my eyes to see how
beautifully and tenderly You have created all
that sustains us. Help me notice and value all
You have made and join the eternal song of
praise. Amen.*

2
Introducing Maria

As the overture fades, we see a single figure racing across the hill, a young woman running with arms stretched wide; delighting in the place she calls her own. She twirls and swirls and sings, delighting in being alive and in that place.

Yes, it is a show, a film, but hopefully we too can pinpoint moments and memories when our hearts brimmed over with joy; wanting to, literally or metaphorically, dance and sing in the sunshine and laugh at the joy of being alive.

From the biggest of opening scenes with its expansive vista, we now zoom in to look at one person. We have swooped down from above those soaring mountains to see the face of a one woman. This change of focus reminds us how important each person is; to our shared humanity and to God. For each individual person is known by Him across all of time and within all of creation.

'God *is* love' (1 John 4:16, my italics). So, with His whole being, He loves the whole of His creation – every single micro element. And within that, God loves us all too; every single 'you' and every single 'me', as if we were the only one alive. We are truly individual and precious to

Him among the billions of people who have ever lived, or indeed who will ever live.

Each one of us is created to be utterly unique. Never before has there been another you or me. Never before did anyone, never again will anyone, share the generational history, the genes, the characteristics, experiences, gifts, abilities and foibles that make each one of us exactly who we are. Like Maria alone on that huge, empty Austrian hill, we are reminded that we are each a beloved, individual person in God's eyes.

This is quite mind-blowing! How can God be big enough to make the whole universe with all His holiness and power, yet bother with the detail of knowing one little person like me? Surely, I am too insignificant, too small to be noticed? Surely, beyond His bothering, especially when so many people in the world appear to need Him more than I do?

Yet perhaps it is His very holiness, power and hugeness that makes it possible for His God-sized heart to love each one of us… *as if we were the only one*? We read in the unfolding narrative of creation, 'So God created humankind in his image, in the image of God he created them; male and female he created them' (Genesis 1:27).

That we are made in His image suggests we are not merely an addendum to creation, but the pinnacle of it. That is a humbling thought, as Psalm 8 says:

> When I look at your heavens, the work of your
>   fingers,
> the moon and the stars that you have established;
> what are human beings that you are mindful of
>   them,

mortals that you care for them?
Yet you have made them a little lower than God,
and crowned them with glory and honour.
You have given them dominion over the works of
    your hands;
you have put all things under their feet,
all sheep and oxen,
and also the beasts of the field,
the birds of the air, and the fish of the sea,
whatever passes along the paths of the seas.
(Psalm 8:3-8)

We can try to reconcile ourselves to the colossal vastness of God's ability to know and love us, but it is difficult to truly comprehend. Thankfully, Jesus understood that we need help to grasp this vital truth as He explained to His disciples:

Are not two sparrows sold for a penny? Yet not one of them will fall to the ground unperceived by your Father. And even the hairs of your head are all counted. So do not be afraid; you are of more value than many sparrows.
(Matthew 10:29-31)

That is the promise and message of God throughout the Bible, from Genesis to Revelation. That is the promise and purpose of Jesus, and that is the wonder of being created and loved by our Creator.

Moments for musing

When we accept that God has both the power to create everything *and* the love to care for everything, that can change how we think of ourselves and our place in His world. How might you reflect upon that?

How might you share that message that with others?

Can you find images and information about our incredible, huge, beautiful world and the billions of people who live in it? Perhaps in books, natural history programmes or other resources? And then remind yourself that you are alive, unique and created 'for just such a time as this' (Esther 4:14).

Prayer

Dear Lord, I find it hard to grasp how
intimately I am known and loved by You.
Please help me to glimpse more of this and live
in that truth. Amen.

3
My Heart Wants to Sing

Maria cannot help but sing while running across her mountain, for her heart is brimming with joy. Hopefully we experience such moments when we may find ourselves whistling, humming or singing, content with life and happily pottering. It's definitely a good day in our house when my husband is singing with gusto; a sign that everything is all right in his world, and therefore mine!

All too often, communal singing has been relegated to school music lessons, Sunday church services or football terraces. It is too easy to get out of the habit of singing; like a muscle we do not use. We can forget to sing... even when alone and no one is listening. Thankfully, many now have realised the benefits of singing for both physical and mental health. The recent growth of community choirs explodes the myth that singing is only for those who are brilliantly, innately musical. Music and singing exercise the brain, the body and the soul. They release endorphins, stress-relieving hormones, and a good old singsong, whether a solo in the shower or as part of a choir, fuels a refreshing feeling of well-being.

It seems that every culture sings; every generation has sung. We become united in song when celebrating or commiserating. David, the king of Israel around 1,000 years before Jesus' birth, was a gifted musician. We read in the first book of Samuel how, as a young shepherd boy, he soothed the tormented King Saul by playing his harp. Then later, having become king after Saul's death, David was renowned for his exuberant worship of the Lord (see, for example, 2 Samuel 6:12-16). He was a prolific writer of scriptural poems and songs expressing the whole gamut of human emotion. For instance, in Psalm 101:1 we read how he sings to his God, 'I will sing of loyalty and justice; to you, O LORD, I will sing.' And again in Psalm 108:

> My heart is steadfast, O God, my heart is steadfast;
> I will sing and make melody.
> Awake, my soul!
> Awake, O harp and lyre!
> I will awake the dawn.
> I will give thanks to you, O LORD, among the peoples,
> And I will sing praises to you among the nations.
> For your steadfast love is higher than the heavens,
> and your faithfulness reaches to the clouds.
> (Psalm 108:1-4)

David understood that singing can release our emotions and give an opportunity to voice our deepest yearnings. Singing expresses joy and soothes lament, and is an expression of praise, a gateway into the peace and presence of God. So singing can be the best thing to do, especially when we do not feel like singing. It might seem contrary to raise a joyful tune when feeling sad or grumpy; yet in those tough moments, music and singing can transform our mood and raise our spiritual barometer.

I know that when I choose praise and worship music on my smart speaker, or a worship CD in the car, I move into a different place spiritually and emotionally; a place where I am reminded that He is with me after all, waiting and willing to minister His healing and encouragement. Singing reminds me *who* I am worshipping; that I am joining heaven's eternal choir. I am reminding myself that God is on His throne and worthy of such praise. Suddenly my issues feel so much more manageable.

Maria sang on that mountaintop because her heart was filled with joy. But later, we discover she's been previously chastised for dancing, specifically waltzing on the way to Mass, and whistling on the stairs. So I wonder… was that waltzing and whistling an overflow of exuberant joy, or was she trying to raise her spirits to meet God because she was feeling in need of His encouragement? Who knows…

Moments for musing

How might you use music and singing to express your feelings and sustain you, especially when things are challenging?

Where might you find more resources for worship/ inspirational music to use in your home, car, etc?

What secular songs inspire you and lift your spirits? Which secular songs 'cross over' into worship when we sing them to God?

Prayer

Dear Lord, help me choose to sing my praises to You, even when I don't feel like it. Amen.

4
When My Heart is Lonely

Maria's day on the mountain has ended; but might there be a hint her cheerful song was more a plea for peace? Was she grappling with an inner dilemma when she sang of the deep shadows and loneliness in her heart?

Perhaps this exuberant girl is struggling with her vocation and questioning her call to the convent? We gather from the film's next scene that she appears to be like a square peg in a round hole. Can she really continue as a postulant with the strict rules of silence and obedience?

Struggling with any important decision is tough, especially when it may be a life-changing one. And although we might not share Maria's particular dilemma, we inevitably face challenges and struggles at times. Those times of doubt, turmoil and decision can feel really dark and lonely, as thoughts churn and drag us into an emotional downward spiral.

Some people are able to talk such things out, processing aloud their dilemma. They need to verbalise their thoughts before they can understand what they are thinking. Others are happier to reflect and ponder quietly, working things out in their own heads before speaking their conclusion. Neither is right or wrong because we are all different. And, however we are wired, we can seek godly wisdom and ask people to pray with us. We don't necessarily need an instant answer or a quick fix, but support along the way as we discern God's guidance.

Because we are made in the image of God (see Genesis 1:27), we are designed to be in relationship with each other as well as with Him. So finding someone to help us hear God's heart and encouragement is one excellent reason why it's good to belong to a church. In a church community, we can find friends who become like family, to give and receive mutual spiritual, emotional and practical support.

I cannot be alone in admitting it's too easy to resort to unhealthy means of consolation when stressed or overwhelmed. That might include bottling things up then splurging on an unsuspecting partner; or seeking to blot things out with a glut of chips or chocolate, or other avoidance tactics. Like all of us, God's people throughout the Bible have frequently needed calming down and reassuring; even the most saintly of biblical and historical saints needed encouragement. One healthier way to cope with wobbles is to stop and quieten both the external and the internal clamouring and to rest in God's presence: Psalm 46:10 puts it this way: 'Be still, and know that I am God!'

Finding that place of peace can take some practice. Moreover, it's not just a scriptural recommendation; the benefits of taking a quiet moment to regroup are widely recognised within mindfulness and meditation practices. It seems that our well-being gurus have caught up with God's ancient principles! And even if we do not 'feel' anything in our stillness, the truth is God has promised to never leave us or forsake us (see Hebrews 13:5). Which means we never have to 'go and find Him' because He's not gone anywhere. Yet that quiet moment can make the space so that we can recognise His presence.

Maria was not a failure in her struggles any more than we are. All of us need encouragement, comfort and direction at some time, as the psalmist wrote:

> Why are you cast down, O my soul,
> and why are you disquieted within me?
> Hope in God; for I shall again praise him,
> my help and my God.
> (Psalm 42:5-6)

For Maria, this mountain was like her home. It was her holy space, her place of refreshment as she grew from childhood to womanhood. So, not surprisingly, it is where she returns to recharge her emotional batteries and seek answers. When we seek His peace, and return to God's Word, then we too can be reminded of His love and refreshment. 'God is ... a very present help in trouble' (Psalm 46:1), and you can't say, or sing, better than that.

Moments for musing

How different might life be if we made seeking God's help our first priority instead of our last resort?

What is your coping system when feeling stressed, lonely or discouraged? What other strategies might you consider too?

What words in Scripture encourage you when you feel troubled? Why not write these out and stick them up where you can see them?

When have you experienced God's presence and faithfulness?

Prayer
*Dear Lord, thank You that You will never
leave me nor forsake me. Help me seek my
solace in You first, and not as a last resort.*
Amen.

5
Faith and Doubts

From the majesty and space of the mountains, we now enter the abbey, to see the nuns in the chapel looking very solemn. Emotionally and visually, it's a very different scene from Maria swirling and singing her way across the green meadows.

Along the cloister, three senior nuns are walking and talking. They are greeted by a breathless Sister Bernice, who has a problem. She has lost Maria, even though she has searched all the usual places. Reverend Mother smiles and suggests that as it's Maria, she should look somewhere unusual. (A bit like when I've lost my car keys and find them in the fridge?)

Sometimes what, or who, we are looking for definitely cannot be found where or when we expect it. And that is even more true about God than it is for car keys! The wonder of God is that we can discover Him in any and every place, and in any and every situation, however unusual. Like the day Jesus was born, not into a royal palace but into a smelly animal shelter. It was no coincidence that the angels announced His birth and called Him Jesus, which means 'the Lord saves', and Emmanuel, which means 'God with us' (Matthew 1:23).

So today, we shouldn't be surprised to find Him 'with us' in unexpected places; and certainly not limited to Sundays or church.

As Reverend Mother gives Sister Bernice this suggestion, she is then challenged by the Mistress of Novices to seriously reconsider Maria's future in the abbey. Quite quickly, we can see that Reverend Mother is an astute woman, and she assures Sister Berthe that she always tries to keep faith in her doubts. She is facing a challenge about Maria's future and will not be easily swayed until she has all the facts. The abbess walks across the courtyard to seek further insight about Maria from her colleagues who are eager to give their opinion. Sister Agatha is definitely in two minds about Maria because she is easy to like, except when she's not!

Like Reverend Mother, we too need to gather wise opinions, as well as draw from our own experiences when facing difficult decisions. Doubts and decisions are part of life and faith. Indeed, faith is based upon a presumption held in the certainty of hope, as the writer to the Hebrews reminds us: 'Now faith is the assurance of things hoped for, the conviction of things not seen' (Hebrews 11:1).

Doubt and faith become the joint doorways through which we walk to discover any answer. We first need to ask the question. Little in life is certain, except perhaps that old cliché of 'death and taxes'.[3] If we never doubted or debated, we would be like automatons, robots programmed to fulfil pre-set actions and commands. And that, most definitely, is not how God created us. We are delightfully, wonderfully, awesomely human, with an

---

[3] Attributed to Benjamin Franklin in 1789.

enquiring mind and an emotional heart and free will to decide.

By thinking and feeling our way through doubts and decisions, we can discover the seemingly impossible, the unseen, the potential and wonder of life and faith. We need doubts to help us question and discern those truths. It is those who are willing to confess their doubts before God who are more likely to journey towards an answer. Those without any questions or doubts could become arrogant or blinkered. They can fail to see the value of wrestling with challenging issues or seeing the world from a different perspective. I recognise that it is through grappling with big issues and difficult dilemmas that I've learned more about myself and God. Faith itself stems from a lack of definitive proof, yet as we take a step of faith, then we discover the truth and recognise the certainty we seek.

Christians believe in faith that there is an unseen but very real and present person, the Holy Spirit who is God Himself. He is one part of the mysterious Trinity of God who, together as Father, Son and Holy Spirit, spoke into the void and sparked the 'Big Bang' for all life to begin. That same, eternal Holy Spirit is still with us and working in the world to draw all people to Himself. That same Holy Spirit is the one who shaped Jesus' own life and actions; the same Holy Spirit who spoke life into Jesus' corpse in the Easter tomb.

So, if we accept that God's Spirit is living with us and in us, then we too, like Reverend Mother, can expect to glean His grace and wisdom when we seek answers. The story then unfolds to reveal how that faith and doubt is fulfilled for Maria and all involved.

Moments for musing

How might you seek the wisdom of God to ask and answer those difficult questions in life?

How might you live within that uncomfortable space when there are unresolved differences with those you love?

How open are you to hearing different opinions, and seeking God's opinion?

Prayer

Dear Lord, thank You that You are with me in my doubts and questions, as well as in my certainties and faith. Be the revealer of wisdom and truth as I discover more about You, our invisible but very present 'God with us'. Amen.

6
Solving a Problem Like Maria

How will they solve a problem like Maria...? This is the question posed by a group of nuns bemoaning Maria's behaviour. Maria is clearly not on the shortlist for Postulant of the Year Award. Her 'faults' appear many and varied and her progress in nun etiquette seems faltering and flawed. Apparently, she climbs trees, tears her dress and her knees get all scraped. Shocking misdemeanours, it seems, along with wearing curlers underneath her wimple and waltzing and whistling at unacceptable moments. Not exactly major crimes but unacceptable in 1930s abbey life – although it wasn't all negative in Maria's virtual report book, as Sister Margaretta admits that Maria makes her laugh.

She is not getting it right; perhaps because she is a postulant – an apprentice, which means she's still learning what it means to be a nun. Like every person learning a new career or skill, she will inevitably make mistakes. We know how easy it is to become critical or judgemental of others when they get things wrong (see Matthew 7:1-5)! Mistakes, though, are not to be feared but embraced, if we can learn from them.

Think of a child learning to walk; they start one step at a time, repeatedly falling over and reverting to shuffling or crawling. Yet at their first inclination to stand, we encourage them to find their balance and delight over those first steps.

Then day by day, month by month, the child learns to toddle one step, two steps, until they manage a comical tottering across the room as all watch, cheer and clap. The child beams, understanding they have achieved something brilliant before inevitably bumping down. Thank goodness for bulky nappies to soften landings! We don't chastise them for falling down but scoop them up with a cheery 'upsy-daisy' and encourage them to start all over again.

I remember my first faltering steps when I became a Christian. There were so many things that I said or did that did not reflect what was 'proper' or positive; simple things like standing up in church when others were sitting, singing the wrong tune, saying the wrong response to prayers, giggling uncontrollably at the communion rail (and that was when I was a curate). It took a while to learn that gossiping about someone is unkind, being critical is judgemental... Fortunately, I was in a church that encouraged and accepted me as I learned. I am still learning.

No one gets everything right, but we must be committed to being teachable and eager to grow in faith and character. God is with us on the adventure, and it takes a lifetime. Like everyone else, I am a work in progress. We cannot earn our way into God's good books by getting things right all the time. Our acceptance and significance in His eyes is solely because of God's grace (His unearned favour), not our efforts.

> God, who is rich in mercy, out of the great love with which he loved us even when we were dead through our trespasses, made us alive together with Christ – by grace you have been saved.
> (Ephesians 2:4-5)

Peter was the disciple who really knew what it was to keep stumbling and getting back up again! He wrote this to encourage us to develop and grow in faith:

> His divine power has given us everything needed for life and godliness, through the knowledge of him who called us by his own glory and goodness … For this very reason, you must make every effort to support your faith with goodness, and goodness with knowledge, and knowledge with self-control, and self-control with endurance, and endurance with godliness, and godliness with mutual affection, and mutual affection with love. For if these things are yours and are increasing among you, they keep you from being ineffective and unfruitful in the knowledge of our Lord Jesus Christ.
> (2 Peter 1:3, 5-8)

Those catchy song lyrics about Maria being a problem to be solved trouble me somewhat. You see, Maria was not the problem. She was keen to discover the right way to become a nun, but despite persevering, she kept missing the mark. Learning any new skill takes perseverance and effort, and there is no shame for those who stumble while they keep trying. And anyway, sometimes it can be the teacher at fault rather than the pupil!

Maybe we too have labelled others or ourselves as a failure or 'the problem', but that is never God's way. Whether it is training novices to become nuns, raising children, or dealing with anyone, in fact, it is important to separate the behaviour from the person. I remember trying to stick to that notion when my children were growing up; they may have done 'naughty things' – but they themselves weren't inherently 'naughty'. What they *did* was separate from *who they were*.

Maria was never 'the problem'. We too can remember who we are, a beloved child of God, and learn to be gentle with ourselves as we learn to become more like Him. Meanwhile, despite each stumble, He will pick us up, again and again and again…

Moments for musing

What particular skill have you developed over the years?

Do you ever feel judged by other people? How does that compare with God's kind and holy judgement?

How might you judge other people? What might that say about your own expectations and attitudes?

Prayer
*Dear Lord, please help me to see myself as
You do, as a precious child learning to live in
Your image. Amen.*

7
A Flibbertigibbet

The nuns have been laying their case about Maria's future before Reverend Mother. As they sing, they continue their chorus of frustration, calling her both a darling *and* a demon, a flibbertigibbet, a will o' the wisp and a clown. In those few words, they seem to have pigeonholed Maria as a lost cause and unworthy of her nun's habit.

How easy it is for people to label others! And how easy to label ourselves and so affect our identity and destiny.

Whether it is a nickname or our given name, we rise or fall to its meaning or implications. Maria's name is rooted in the same name as Jesus' mother, Mary, who suggested all generations could call her 'Blessed' because of her role as the mother of the Christ child:

> My soul magnifies the Lord,
> and my spirit rejoices in God my Saviour,
> for he has looked with favour on the lowliness of his
>   servant.
> Surely, from now on all generations will call me
>   blessed;
> for the Mighty One has done great things for me,
> and holy is his name.
> (Luke 1:46-49)

God knows us by our name, and names matter to Him, as we read in the Old Testament: 'Do not fear, for I have redeemed you; I have called you by name, you are mine' (Isaiah 43:1). Often biblical characters were shaped by their name or had their names changed by God to reflect their new role or status. In the Old Testament, Abram's name means 'exalted ancestor'. A few chapters and adventures later, he is renamed by God as Abraham, 'ancestor of a multitude' (Genesis 17:3-8). Those two additional letters lead him to embrace his new name and new role as the father of a whole new nation.

Simon in the New Testament is renamed by Jesus as Peter, meaning the 'rock' (Matthew 16:18), upon whom Jesus will build His Church – although we read in the Gospels how, at times, Peter was anything but a rock. It was only after Pentecost that he really embraced his God-given name. He had been named by Jesus, not for who he was, but for who he would become. Names can shape our future as much as our heritage.

For years, my name, Bryony, was so unusual that I was literally the only Bryony in any school in our town. Being unusual in name meant that I always had to spell my name, explain what it meant and expect to be called almost anything starting with B. I might be called Blodwyn, Bianca, Byrony, Brownie... When asked my name over the years, my reply became somewhat trite as I trotted out the same old explanation, 'No, it's not Welsh; Bryony is a poisonous weed that grows in the hedgerows.'

While that might be truthful about my horticultural namesakes the Black Bryony and White Bryony, it also hinted at something about my perception of who I was; something negative about my whole purpose and identity in life. It wasn't until well into middle age that I recalibrated that negativity after quite a stern heavenly challenge! I was answering the same old question about my 'weedy' name, and gave my stock answer. Into that moment, I felt God say in no uncertain terms, 'Do not call yourself a poisonous weed! You are a beautiful wildflower created by Me, called to blossom where you are planted. You are My precious daughter.'

In that moment, I realised how much I reflected my identity in that derogatory explanation of my name. That day was a powerful renaming of my inner child, from Bryony the Weed to Bryony the Wildflower, and it started to reshape all that I am and all I trust to become in Him.

When we see Maria running into the abbey courtyard, late, disruptive and undisciplined, she does reflect behaviour akin to a 'flibbertigibbet'. But fast forward to the sensitive governess who helps the children to flourish while encouraging their father to emerge from his grief; that woman is definitely no flibbertigibbet or clown. Neither is she a will o' the wisp as she holds the family hiding in the abbey tombs, or walks across the mountains to freedom. Through the power of love, Maria discovers her true identity and leaves behind the old labels to fulfil her divine destiny.

Moments for musing

How much does your given name reflect your identity?

What nicknames or labels have you been given by others or yourself that help or hinder your self-worth?

What difference might it make to embrace the identity that God gives you as His beloved child?

Prayer

Dear Lord, when You called Your Son, Jesus, Emmanuel, 'God with us', it summarised both who He was and what He came to do. Help me remember that I too am Your beloved child.

Amen.

8
Do Let Me Say I'm Sorry

Even though it was decades ago, I remember all too vividly the message from the school office: 'Would Bryony go to the headmistress' study at break time, please?'

Oh, the shame and fear. The trepidation as I lined up alongside other pupils summoned and waiting in the narrow corridor, mentally trawling though the past few days to work out what rule I'd broken. There were multiple reasons for being called into the head's office, not just to be given a dressing down, a detention or worse. Yet for some reason my default emotion was always guilt. It was genuinely misplaced guilt, because I was a real conformist at school and rarely in big trouble. But, on the rare occasion I did stray, then I'd carry the humiliation for weeks or even months.

In the next scene of *The Sound of Music*, we see a much-chastened Maria waiting outside Reverend Mother's study. She is clean and tidy and rather different from the errant girl who scurried across the courtyard and rolled her eyes at her exasperated peers. Maria is now contrite and enters the rather intimidating office to approach Reverend Mother. She sits on the edge of her chair and immediately erupts into explanations and apologies.

Maria explains how she's always in trouble, especially with her mentor. The abbess suppresses a smile as our postulant admits to kissing the ground whenever Sister Berthe appears, to shortcut the inevitable process of scolding and subsequent penitence. However, on this occasion, rather than being summoned for a scolding, there is another reason for the meeting. Yet Maria is so desperate to say sorry, she doesn't give the abbess any chance to speak.

Saying sorry really can make us feel better. It helps shed the guilt that can weigh us down, and can bring huge relief. In my experience, one of the major benefits of having a relationship with God is that ability to leave my guilt with Him. Whether I might feel bad about eating too much pudding and being gluttonous, envying someone's more comfortable lifestyle, being snarky with my husband… or any one of hundred things that mars God's character in me, I need not feel any guilt for past mistakes. There is a certainty in forgiveness being once and for all, as the apostle Paul writes: 'There is therefore now no condemnation for those who are in Christ Jesus' (Romans 8:1).

God is not like a celestial head teacher. He does not summon us for a 'telling-off'. He is not a God of detentions and punishments, but of grace and patience. It is not so much *anger* He expresses as the world goes pear-shaped, as *anguish* at the pain we inflict and experience. It is not shame and fear that we should feel before him, but awe, reverence and gratitude.

There is an oft-quoted Christian adage that God loves us just as we are, but loves us too much to leave us that way. That process of ongoing discipleship means that we are on a journey, and when we get things wrong, then we have the opportunity to recognise and learn from it.

Jesus' final words on the cross, 'It is finished' (John 19:30), heralded a new era of grace and forgiveness for all humanity. As He died, the huge curtain that separated the *Most Holy Place* in the temple 'was torn in two' (Luke 23:45). That tearing of the curtain illustrated there was no longer any barrier separating humanity from the *Most Holy Person*. The gulf that had formed between our holy God and His unholy people was eternally resolved.

Like Maria discovered, it is healthy to recognise when we need to say sorry before others and before God, as John the apostle wrote:

> If we say that we have no sin, we deceive ourselves, and the truth is not in us. If we confess our sins, he who is faithful and just will forgive us our sins and cleanse us from all unrighteousness.
> (1 John 1:8-9)

When we say sorry before God, something of a divine exchange happens. As we offer our confession, so we are invited to accept the free gift of His forgiveness – a two-way exchange. Yet while that forgiveness is a free gift for us, it cost Jesus everything, as we shall read later.

Moments for musing

What prompts you to say sorry to God or someone around you? How do you respond to that prompting?

What's the difference between a challenge from the Holy Spirit to put something right, and condemnation that is definitely not from God?

What does it mean that 'God loves you just as you are, but loves you too much to leave you that way'?

Prayer
Dear Lord, help me to be ready to say sorry to my friends and relatives when I need to, and to forgive others as You have forgiven me.
Amen.

9
Mountains Led Me to You

Back in the study, Maria continues to explain why she was late and singing on the mountain. She describes how the sky was so blue and the Untersberg mountain appeared to be inviting her to go on, higher and higher, right up through the clouds. Reverend Mother is somewhat perturbed and suggests that if it had got dark, she would surely be lost up there?

Maria assures her that couldn't happen for she is so familiar with the mountain. Even as a child she would spend days up there, and on returning would climb the tree that overlooked the abbey. From her vantage point she could watch the sisters working in the garden and hear them singing on the way to prayer, thereby planting the seed for her vocation to serve God.

But it's not just Maria or nuns who have such childhood longings fulfilled. Many people can look back to see how their path in life had early inspirations. A childhood love of playing 'hospitals' or 'schools', perhaps, or taking apart mechanical things and putting them back together, enjoying sports, caring for animals, creative stories, the joy of mathematics... the ways to spot early potential are endless.

I wonder if you have ever stood at the back of a ship and watched the water foaming behind you? You might have noticed the wake stretching behind, showing the route the ship has taken, yet it is impossible to see the way forward marked out in the water.

Jeremiah was an Old Testament prophet whose commission was to warn God's people to turn from their godless ways. However, even as he foretold the terrible consequences of their rebellion, God's bigger picture was always to offer redemption:

> For surely I know the plans I have for you, says the LORD, plans for your welfare and not for harm, to give you a future with hope. Then when you call upon me and come and pray to me, I will hear you. When you search for me, you will find me; if you seek me with all your heart.
> (Jeremiah 29:11-13)

And that divine promise of a hope and future was not just for the ancient Israelites; it is a promise we can all hold on to. God has set into our hearts His divine potential, so we can discover and fulfil His opportunities and gifts. A true vocation and calling can be a paid or an unpaid role, a job or any opportunity where we allow His love to shine in us and through us. And it is definitely not confined to those who wear wimples or dog collars!

Maria's childhood vocational seeds were inspired by the nuns and ultimately by the Holy Spirit. For her, as for us all, it became a journey of discovery, perhaps to take her along paths that would turn out quite differently from that she had envisaged. But that would be a plot spoiler.

God's future plans, however, are known only by Him. Even Jesus, while He lived as a man, could not know absolutely everything. He knew enough of His heavenly Father's plans to fulfil His role, but His humanity temporarily limited His eternal knowledge, as He expressed when teaching about the prophesied fulfilment of God's kingdom:

> Heaven and earth will pass away, but my words will not pass away.
> But about that day and hour no one knows, neither the angels of heaven, nor the Son, but only the Father.
> (Matthew 24:35-36)

Specific knowledge about the future would be too much for us to bear. Indeed, we are cautioned against trying to peer into the future by any method, or trusting those who suggest they have foreknowledge of such things. We are advised to live and trust for today and leave what is to come in God's hands.

God's promises and plans are always good, and as we respond to God's call, there emerges a wonderful weaving together of life and circumstances. Our personality and gifts lead us onwards, for our vocations emerge from our passions and abilities. Our 'doing' will emerge from our 'being'.

A few years ago, my wise friend, Judith, once said when I was questioning which path to take, 'If you want to do God's will, you will do God's will!' and she was so right. Looking back over the years, we can all look behind and see where we've been and how far we've come, seeing the 'wake' of our life (perhaps that's why funeral 'wakes' are so named!). But the way forward, well, that's all down to trust and living by faith with what we have today.

Moments for musing

Psalm 37:4 says that when we 'Take delight in the LORD' He will give us 'the desires of [our] heart'. How might you discover the desires of your heart?

How might we hone our desires to match God's character and purposes?

Looking back in the 'wake' of your life's journey, can you see how God might have been guiding you?

Prayer
*Dear Lord, please help me discover Your best
plans for me. Help me to seek You and find
You with all my heart. Amen.*

10
Don't Send Me Away

Maria is devastated. It has taken years to fulfil her childhood dream of becoming a nun, and here she is, being sent away by Reverend Mother. It feels like a punishment, even though she is being told it is no such thing. For although she has been struggling with the disciplines of convent life, the convent is home, her safe place.

Faced with a mortified Maria, the abbess is not to be swayed. She's experienced enough to know a thing or two about postulants, and about God's will, so offers Maria some wisdom. Now she understands more about what life is like in the convent, going out into the world for this assignment will give her the chance to discover if being a nun really is her true vocation.

Sometimes the hardest challenge is the one to discover the very core of who we are, to discover the unknown depth of our own character. Maria's face indicates her inner turmoil; we can see her repressed instinct to argue. Yet she stays silent. 'Maria?' asks the abbess gently. It is a rhetorical question, one not requiring a reply but offering an opportunity for obedience. One word, which speaks to her soul. 'Maria' – her name.

That moment when Reverend Mother speaks Maria's name echoes another moment 2,000 years ago. It was on that first Easter Sunday and Mary Magdalene was outside the empty tomb, distraught because she thought someone had taken the body of her beloved Jesus (John 20:11-18). Through her tears, Mary saw a man and, thinking He was the gardener, she asked, 'Where have you put Him?' (see v15). Instead of using long explanations to answer her question, the newly resurrected Jesus just said one word: 'Mary' (v16). And offered in that one word, her name, was every answer she needed. By it, Jesus affirmed her identity, His love, her purpose.

Back in the convent, Maria listens to her commission, which is to become the governess to the local von Trapp family. It is no small task. 'Seven children!' she gulps, while attempting an air of nonchalance to ask the reason for the rapid turnover of governesses. 'The Lord will show you in His own good time,' replies the abbess. Maria now understands this is a challenge for her to explore; and to do this she will need to leave the security of the abbey.

Remember Peter, the disciple who left the security of the boat one windy night on Lake Galilee to walk on water:

> And early in the morning he came walking towards them on the lake. But when the disciples saw him walking on the lake, they were terrified, saying, 'It is a ghost!' And they cried out in fear. But immediately Jesus spoke to them and said, 'Take heart, it is I; do not be afraid.'
>
> Peter answered him, 'Lord, if it is you, command me to come to you on the water.' He said, 'Come.'

So Peter got out of the boat, started walking on the water, and came towards Jesus. But when he noticed the strong wind, he became frightened, and beginning to sink, he cried out, 'Lord, save me!' Jesus immediately reached out his hand and caught him, saying to him, 'You of little faith, why did you doubt?' When they got into the boat, the wind ceased. And those in the boat worshipped him, saying, 'Truly you are the Son of God.'
(Matthew 14:25-33)

It is worth reminding ourselves that the disciples' boat, like all boats, was built with the express purpose of floating on top of the water to keep its passengers dry! Peter was an experienced fisherman and knew very well how boats worked. He knew too that the Sea of Galilee was very deep, very cold and prone to unpredictable weather.

It would be somewhat crazy to get out of a boat in the middle of a stormy sea to test the viability of walking on water. Yet that one particular night, as Jesus *walked* across the water towards them, Peter was the one who defied all laws of physics. It was Peter, spontaneous, impetuous Peter, who was the one disciple to step out of that boat, and in doing so, he was anything but crazy!

As Jesus called his name, this fallible yet determined fisherman placed one foot over the edge of the boat, then another, and did what no human had ever done before. He walked on water with Jesus.

Peter had learned enough to know that when Jesus called, He also equipped and enabled. And as long as his eyes were fixed upon Jesus, he was able to do the impossible. As his feet defied the watery depths, we can imagine Peter's brain working overtime: 'This is unreal!' We can imagine his pure elation before realising the utter madness of what he was actually doing! And that's when he took his eyes off Jesus, looked at the waves and the boat floating far from the shore, and glimpsed his incredulous friends watching in open-mouthed astonishment. However, by taking his eyes of Jesus, he panicked. 'Lord, save me!' he cried as the water rushed over his rapidly sinking body. And through the waves the firm hand of his Lord pulled him up to escort him back into the floating boat.

Maria was not being chastised for wearing curlers in her hair or for being late for chapel; she was being expressly assigned a new opportunity. She was being asked to step out of her 'boat', to say yes and trust God as she moved into the unknown.

Like Maria, we all face opportunities to step out in faith. And like Maria and Peter, we may well be challenged to face risky decisions and opportunities. If and when that happens, then through faith we too can trust that when Jesus calls, He equips, and we will always have a choice. Will we stay in our 'comfort zone', our symbolic boat? Or will we accept His commission and step out to discover that He is indeed with us, all the way.

Moments for musing

Is there a metaphorical 'boat' that you might need to step out of?

If we think of being 'commissioned' as accepting a 'co-mission' with Jesus, what might that be like – to be in partnership with Jesus?

Peter responded to Jesus' call before stepping out of the boat. What is the difference between 'stepping out' of the boat when Jesus calls and randomly 'jumping off'? How might you discern the difference?

Prayer

Dear Lord; help me to trust that when You call, You will equip. Please help me recognise, respond and be ready when You call. Amen.

11
Leaving the Abbey

Maria has changed her nuns' habit for day clothes that are definitely more functional than fashionable. She is leaving the abbey to start her new life. As she goes out, we notice on the abbey wall there's a large word written in the stucco: *'Pax'*. It's a poignant reminder that this has been her place of peace, but now she is called to leave it. With guitar and carpetbag in hand, she pauses at the crucifix of Jesus and reassures herself that, as Reverend Mother always says, if the Lord closes a door, He opens a window. Then she turns through the archway and, as the large metal gate clunks behind her, she exits her old life.

I wonder if she is carrying all her worldly goods in those two bags? Her guitar may not have been used too often in the abbey, but it's obviously part of her life, as well as vital to the storyline. But to have everything in that one carpetbag suggests she travels very lightly.

There is an account in the Bible when Jesus sends out His disciples to take God's good news to every local town (Luke 10:1-11). He tells them to travel lightly; perhaps He wants them to trust that God will provide all they need. A little later we read how they joyfully returned with testimonies of power and provision.

When I was fortunate to visit Austria for a special holiday, I made the mistake of overpacking. Big mistake! We were travelling across Europe by rail. All was very exciting until I had to lug suitcases on and off trains and taxis, up and down staircases, and balance precariously on escalators; only then did I realise I'd made a significant, logistical blunder. Every leg of the journey became a battle with suitcases and rucksacks, each one packed with stuff for every conceivable 'just in case' option. Most of what I lugged around was superfluous, and made my journey unnecessarily hard work. I just hope I remember that lesson before embarking on any future trips.

Isn't that the case with our spiritual and emotional baggage too? So much of what we lug around is superfluous and makes things unnecessarily hard work. It is tempting to hold on to grievances, disappointments and anger. But it doesn't need to be like that. Jesus, who knew what it is to be weary and discouraged, offers to be our divine baggage handler. He said, 'Come to me, all you that are weary and are carrying heavy burdens, and I will give you rest' (Matthew 11:28)

Despite that gracious offer, we so often insist on carrying our own baggage instead of allowing God to help. Moreover, why do we continue to hang on to such emotional baggage in the first place when we could leave it at the foot of the cross? The cross at Calvary was in effect our divine, eternal 'Baggage Disposal Point', where Jesus took on Himself all our sins and burdens, so that we don't need to be weighed down by them, or attempt to collect them later.

Not too long after that Austrian trip we moved house, and in preparation had a good clear-out. We sorted through dusty things packed in old boxes that had travelled from garage to garage, loft to loft and then been forgotten about between house moves. We had a mountain of ridiculous things, broken things, extra things that might 'come in handy' one day but never did. Therefore, we decided to only take what was eminently practical, beautiful or sentimental; not a new maxim, I know, but a useful one when sorting through clutter. The rest would go to the charity shop or the tip. (My husband admits he questioned exactly which category he slotted into: practical, beautiful or sentimental!)

That house move with its vigorous decluttering became a liberating experience. Our removal costs were cheaper because we needed a smaller van, and packing and unpacking was much easier. However, perhaps most importantly, we realised that what we now owned was what we treasured, precious things that both enriched and sustained us. We could look forward without the clutter, trusting God would provide all we needed.

Of course, there is nothing wrong with having lovely and practical things. We are not all called to the simplicity of a nun's life. But what we do possess needs to count, to matter enough to be important, useful, cherished and intentional.

Maria appeared to own very little, but she had everything she needed because she had faith. That faith would remind her that when a metaphorical door closes, God is perfectly capable of opening a metaphorical window to open up the best way forward.

Moments for musing

Do you carry any 'baggage' that might be better left with Jesus at the foot of the cross?

Have you got 'stuff' that you hang on to but don't really *need*?

Refugees face a stark choice about what to leave and what to take when fleeing from their homes. What might you take if you only had one bag in each hand?

Prayer

Dear Lord, help me leave my burdens and baggage with You and not be tempted to grab them back. I pray for a healthy relationship with my possessions to truly appreciate all that I have. Amen.

12
I Have Confidence

As she leaves the abbey, Maria starts to sing. Her song starts slowly and thoughtfully, more of a melodious pondering than a rousing chorus. This assignment is going to be a bigger deal than she first realised. She asks herself why, having always yearned for adventures, is she suddenly so scared? She voices the self-doubt we all face at times.

It's good to listen to the lyrics as she wavers back and forth, working through her doubts. How on earth is she going to connect and cope with a captain with seven children? But something quite wonderful happens as she continues. She expresses that inner journey from fear to faith. What starts tentatively builds to become a rally cry of confidence; a declaration to herself and the world that all would be well, despite what may lie ahead.

We can all identify with that struggle: questioning ourselves – why am I so scared, or am I up to the job? And on top of those doubts come the plagues of 'what ifs' that cripple our confidence and pollute our peace.

Right now, as I write this, I am sitting on a chair. I actually didn't think twice before plonking myself down on it because I had confidence this chair would hold me. It has fulfilled its purpose before, so no reason to expect otherwise today. Why would I be plagued by 'what ifs' every time I sit on it? (I need to add an aside here and explain why I actually have a good reason *not* to trust all chairs. On my fifteenth birthday, dressed in my best 1970s floaty dress at the local disco, I intended to impress. I danced the niftiest moves, kept my lip gloss shiny and then took my non-alcoholic apple juice to recline on a chair at the edge of the dance floor. Only it didn't go as I expected… in a moment of horror I disappeared through the seat, which had been mischievously tampered with. As my bum hit the floor, my legs flew skyward in the most unflattering way. Needless to say, after being hauled out by sniggering friends, it took a while to trust chairs again. I don't think I was the deliberate target for the prank; I just picked the spoof chair.)

Chairs and practical jokes aside, let's return to the issue of confidence. Thirty years ago, just three months after becoming a Christian, I discovered I was expecting a baby. And while that was wonderful news, it was tinged with some concern, because I'd previously experienced three miscarriages and the neonatal death of a baby born with a congenital heart condition. For me, having a 'successful' outcome to a pregnancy was anything but a foregone conclusion.

Around week nine of my pregnancy, I was at church and asked someone to pray for me. As they prayed, I was enveloped by a deep sense of peace; I knew beyond doubt that it would be all right. I didn't know whether 'all right' meant the safe delivery of a healthy baby, or if 'all right' meant that if things did go wrong, God would take me through it and give me the strength to cope.

My doctors were professional and competent. My midwives were sympathetic and caring, but none of them could actually guarantee to deliver a successful outcome. And, as much as friends comforted me with, 'I'm sure it will be all right this time,' and doctors said, 'You're worrying because of your past history,' no one in my care team could actually *promise* it would be OK.

I sailed though that pregnancy with an unbelievable sense of joy and peace, despite the odds stacked against us. When I delivered a healthy baby son, we named him Joshua. It was the name we believed God had given us for our baby. (Bear with me for another aside in this story... God had given us a boy's name, which was strange because I was convinced my bump would be a girl and was thinking about calling her Emily or Elizabeth. My instincts had been correct with my previous pregnancies, but on this occasion God was, unsurprisingly, correct! He knew my son before I did.)

The point of my story is less about a 'successful outcome', for which I am eternally grateful, but more the discovery of a real and new confidence in God that carried me through that pregnancy. I learned the difference between hoping and trusting, and the futility of worry.

Now, no one really likes an overconfident person, someone who over-promises and under-delivers. That is misplaced arrogance and not the same as having confidence in God, which is based on His ability to deliver, not ours. He never over-promises and under-delivers. The writer of the book of Hebrews reminds us why we can have this confidence, this boldness to trust God:

Since, then, we have a great high priest who has passed through the heavens, Jesus, the Son of God, let us hold fast to our confession. For we do not have a high priest who is unable to sympathize with our weaknesses, but we have one who in every respect has been tested as we are, yet without sin. Let us therefore approach the throne of grace with boldness, so that we may receive mercy and find grace to help in time of need.
(Hebrews 4:14-16)

The message is simple and profound. Because Jesus was both fully God and fully man, His divinity means He understands everything with the power to act as necessary; yet because He lived on earth, He also shares and understands our humanity. Because of all that, we can have real confidence in our real God, and as God's beloved children, we are invited to approach 'the throne of grace' and ask for His help.

That is the basis for the confidence Maria sings about. She sings that, whether it's rainy or sunny in life, God is with us in every circumstance. She sings of that biblical confidence that she can 'do all things through him who strengthens [her]' (Philippians 4:13); no wonder her song is such a rousing call to positivity.

Moments for musing

Where do you usually place your confidence when events look uncertain or you need help?

What might it mean to accept that God is on His 'throne of grace' and ready and willing to hear and help you?

What Bible verses could you find and write out to keep as reminders of this truth?

Prayer

Dear Lord, thank You that I am welcomed
before Your throne of grace. Please give me
the confidence to approach You, knowing that
You are both willing to hear and able to help.
Amen.

13
Strength Doesn't Lie in Numbers

Maria has left the abbey, taken the bus from Salzburg and is now walking towards the von Trapp family house. Although, actually, she doesn't walk as such, but runs and sings along the lane. She's brimming with renewed confidence as her new adventure unfolds. Her song echoes that God-given promise, that even after the darkest of times, spring will come again.

Maria swings her bag and guitar filled with this new confidence, although her bag does look deceptively light and easy to swing! However, in real life, many of us would find it too hard to 'swing our bags' along the road of life. Sometimes we do not even have the strength to put one foot in front of the other, much less skip along the road and swing even an empty bag.

I have a Bible verse on my wall that has carried me through such tough times. In it, God tells His people:

> Do not fear, for I am with you,
> do not be afraid, for I am your God;
> I will strengthen you, I will help you,
> I will uphold you with my victorious right hand.
> (Isaiah 41:10)

It's a pertinent reminder that the King of all kings is with me. That His 'right hand' is holding, guiding and sustaining me with all His strength. And that promise is echoed in the next line of Maria's song as she declares that we don't find our strength in numbers (unless the number is the One true, living God!) and we don't find our strength in wealth. How true!

The psalmist summarises it well: 'The LORD is my strength and my shield; in him my heart trusts' (Psalm 28:7). Threaded throughout the Bible is the wonderful truth that whenever we are weary or worn down, God can give us the strength to stand up for what is important, to keep going and find hope beyond our troubles. Maria's hope is captured within the next sentence of that same psalm: '… so I am helped, and my heart exults, and with my song I give thanks to him.'

Help to cope with heavy loads can come in a variety of different ways… Before he retired, my husband sold forklift trucks. It was a bit of a conversation dampener when people asked, for it wasn't the most glamorous job in the world. Until I met him, I had never given a second thought to a single forklift truck. I had no idea how vital these trucks are to the worldwide economy. I soon learned that virtually everything we have in our houses, shops and factories depends on being moved at some time on a forklift truck.

Some are huge machines, some much smaller and designed for tight spaces, yet all are designed to be strong and agile. They are without doubt indispensable in both manufacturing and distribution sectors. Forklift trucks carry the loads that people can't. What would take a person all day to shift can be done in minutes by a forklift truck. It trundles in and gently manoeuvres its forks under the load before effortlessly moving it to the correct place. It can reach higher and carry heavier loads than human arms ever could. It can keep going all day when human energy would flag. It just does what it is designed to do. The combined skill of the truck designer and operator working together have solved the logistical problem of moving cumbersome things.

And although it might not be the most obvious analogy, so it is with God. We can rely on His strength, for God's strength is wrapped up in His whole character and purpose. He won't have an off day, be grumpy with us and withdraw His favour. His purpose is to love and support us, to work with us and bear the weight of the world. He will not break down, as a forklift truck might, or run out of fuel. God is dependable and sure, so when we cannot carry our load any more, He will, and He works with us to achieve more than we could ever alone.

Maria continues her song, singing that after a night of peaceful slumber it's good to wake up, and wake up well. I mentioned that sign in my bedroom from Isaiah 41; it is actually right opposite my bed, so when I emerge blurry-eyed it is usually the first thing I see as I wake up; a reminder for the day ahead; a reminder that when situations or tasks might appear daunting, or when the occasional dark mood needs shifting, I am not alone.

Maria's song is packed full of beautiful analogies about trust, and her penultimate line echoes more biblical truths reflected in the book of Isaiah:

> Those of steadfast mind you keep in peace –
> in peace because they trust in you.

Trust in the LORD for ever,
for in the LORD GOD
you have an everlasting rock.
(Isaiah 26:3-4)

With that hope of God's strength, Maria is walking in renewed trust that He is more than able to help her, and that makes her heart sing. No wonder she can sing that she has confidence!

Moments for musing

What makes you feel strong and courageous?

What Bible verse would be a good one to greet you each morning?

Maria sang about trust... but for many people, trust in people, or even in the institution of Church, has been broken. How might you learn to trust again if you've been hurt or let down?

We trust that God will never let us down, but sometimes His help and presence are not apparent or instant; how might we keep going in those times?

Prayer
Dear Lord, You are our everlasting rock; help me to remember and trust You even when I feel joyless, weak and vulnerable. Amen.

14
Oh Help!

Maria is bursting with confidence as she heads towards her new vocation. That is, until she catches her first glimpse of the imposing von Trapp family house. Peering through its huge gates, her cheerful singing dies on her lips, until all we can hear is a bird singing in the background. Will she turn tail and run back to the convent? Thankfully, she doesn't; but it must be tempting. In the silence before the imposing house, she murmurs, 'Oh help.'

She gulps and appears to wrestle with the twin truths she faces. She has no obvious training and is inexperienced for her new role, yet she trusts God is with her. Then, with resolute determination, Maria reaches for the heavy latch and opens the gate. She starts to walk towards the front door, picking up the theme of her confidence song... then, gathering speed, she runs across the courtyard to arrive breathlessly at the rather grand front door.

Like Maria, we too will face those 'oh help' moments. Moments when those two words will be the only words we can utter. And in those moments, those two words will surely be the only prayer necessary. Prayers don't have to be long and complex for God to hear. Sometimes the best prayers are the short, honest ones. What matters is that in our desperation, we are turning to Him.

Jesus taught His disciples some fundamental truths about prayer. Primarily it is about relationship; a loving relationship between our heavenly Father and His beloved children. He taught us that prayer begins by acknowledging and accepting both who He is and who we are, which is why the prayer Jesus taught His disciples begins, 'Our Father' (Matthew 6:9-13). By faith, those two words alone remind us we share the same heavenly Father as Jesus.

Jesus also taught that those in a real relationship with God do not need to jump through theological hoops or make a public display of their prayers. He certainly didn't win friends among the religious elite of His day when He admonished those prone to a show of lengthy prayers. Their prayers, He suggested, were more about grandstanding than reflecting their love for God:

> And whenever you pray, do not be like the hypocrites; for they love to stand and pray in the synagogues and at the street corners, so that they may be seen by others. Truly I tell you, they have received their reward. But whenever you pray, go into your room and shut the door and pray to your Father who is in secret; and your Father who sees in secret will reward you.
>
> When you are praying, do not heap up empty phrases as the Gentiles do; for they think that they will be heard because of their many words. Do not be like them, for your Father knows what you need before you ask him.
>
> (Matthew 6:5-8)

We read in the Gospels how Jesus responded to those who were desperate. Rather than being moved by pious indignation or self-pity, He responded to the simplest acts or words expressed by people in need.

As Jesus was on His final journey to Jerusalem, He was followed, as usual, by large crowds. Among them were two blind men begging by the roadside. They shouted as He passed by, 'Lord, have mercy on us, Son of David' (Matthew 20:29-34). In those eight words, they expressed a simple but profound faith: that not only was Jesus their Lord, but that the Lord was present and able to help them. Jesus asked them what they specifically wanted. 'Lord, let our eyes be opened,' they replied.

I suggest that by asking them what they wanted, Jesus wanted them to verbalise their needs – not because He didn't actually know. Jesus understood that sometimes it is only by voicing our need that we fully own our request. Their simple, short prayer expressed faith and changed their lives, for, filled with compassion and power, Jesus immediately healed them before continuing on His way towards the cross.

Sometimes, though, even a short sentence was unnecessary for Jesus to respond. Another Gospel account tells of a woman who had been ill for twelve years (Mark 5:25-34). Because of her condition, she was an outcast in society and had spent all her money on doctors who had failed to help. She was truly desperate and, knowing Jesus was in town, was anxious to reach Him. She flagrantly ignored every social rule to fight her way through the crowd, and with silent determination reached out to touch the hem of His cloak. In that act of faith, that wordless prayer, she appealed silently and desperately for healing.

At her touch, Jesus turned to the woman; those watching probably expected Him to be angry at her audacity, but instead Jesus addressed her as 'daughter' (v34). In His response to her appeal He affirmed both His compassion and His healing through that simple act of faith.

Like any human relationship, our relationship with God depends on and deepens through two-way communication, both spoken and unspoken. We have God's Word in the Bible and the Holy Spirit to inspire us and reveal His character. In response we are invited to express our deepest hopes and dreams before Him. We are called into a genuine dialogue fuelled by faith.

We pray and ask for His help, but not because He does not know what is going on in our life – because as the psalmist writes, God knows us even better than we know ourselves:

> O LORD, you have searched me and known me.
> You know when I sit down and when I rise up;
> you discern my thoughts from far away.
> You search out my path and my lying down,
> and are acquainted with all my ways.
> Even before a word is on my tongue,
> O LORD, you know it completely.
> (Psalm 139:1-4)

We are invited to articulate – to think or cry out our thoughts and prayers to help us verbalise what we need while declaring our relationship with Him. Praying is so much more than a shopping list of requests; it is an expression of faith that helps to build an eternal relationship with our living God.

'Oh help!' Maria says. When all we can say before God is, 'Oh help,' there is no better prayer in the universe.

Moments for musing

While we don't need long and involved prayers to form or maintain a relationship with God, like any relationship, we need to invest time in it. What might help your relationship with God go even deeper?

What inspires you about how Jesus lived in relationship with His heavenly Father?

When we pray, we are seeking God's help to intervene or change a situation. Sometimes He does that through human acts of kindness. How might you be the answer to someone's 'Oh help'?

What makes a prayer, a prayer?

Prayer
Dear Lord, thank You that You know me even better than I know myself. Please help me to be honest when I pray. Amen.

15
First Impressions

Maria knocks on the door of the von Trapp house and it is opened by the butler, Franz. He is clearly less than impressed by her appearance, or her arrival, and reluctantly ushers her into the palatial hallway to wait. In silent awe she gazes around, impressed by the splendour of her new surroundings. She's keen to explore, and wanders off to peer through a rather imposing door into a huge, gilded ballroom. It is empty and unused, with dustsheets covering remnants of furniture. Uninvited, she enters this magnificent room and, in a moment of make-believe, curtseys before an imaginary dance partner. In the next minute, her daydreaming is suddenly interrupted by Captain von Trapp, who has flung open the door. As Maria scuttles out, he orders her to never enter that hallowed room again. Back in the hallway, they scrutinise each other before he demands why she appears to be staring at him.

She explains that he doesn't look much like a sea captain before he retorts that she doesn't look like a governess. They appear to have got off to a rather bad start.

They say you never get a second chance to make a first impression. Like it or not, first impressions do count, even though sometimes we wish they didn't. Psychologists suggest we all make snap judgements and split-second conclusions about someone's character, capability and social status upon that first glance. We do, literally and metaphorically, judge books by their cover.

Maria and the captain's next conversation does little to assuage those inauspicious first impressions. With some feistiness, Maria refuses to be summoned by his whistle, unlike his children who have been trained to respond to their individual call signal that he blows on his boatswain's pipe. He might be a naval sea captain, but she has just won their first battle, and the stage is set for their ensuing relationship. While it is very tempting to judge by appearances, they can be so wrong, as these two eventually discover.

Today I ate an apple… well, I shared an apple with my husband. There was just one left in the fruit bowl and it looked a bit scabby so I let him have it while I opted for the biscuit tin. When he cut it open, it was surprisingly sweet and juicy inside and tasted much better than it looked. Inside that scabby apple was something else very special that no one had ever seen before… for inside the apple was a star. The secret star-shaped seedpod that contained the pips with the potential for the next generation of apple trees. Until we'd cut that apple in half, it had been hidden from the world, growing in secret. The outside looked less than appealing, but inside, not only was the apple tasty, but it also held the promise of the next generation. And because my hubby is selfless and kind, he shared it with me. I know I didn't really deserve it, but I guess that is grace in action!

While the propensity to judge by first impressions is a human trait, it is not reflective of God's character. The Bible is full of unlikely looking champions of faith, who all belied first impressions. Even Jesus didn't much look like the promised Messiah. In fact, most people who lived then were anything but excited about His birth, His methods or His message. The Jewish people desperately anticipated a Messiah, and messiahs were not supposed to look like a lowly carpenter.

A thousand years before Jesus, we read how the prophet Samuel was sent to Jesse's house in Bethlehem to seek and anoint the next king of Israel. That was a risky mission for Samuel because the current king, Saul, was still on the throne. Sadly, King Saul, Israel's first king, turned out to be a bad one. One by one, Jesse's seven strapping sons were each presented to Samuel. The prophet sought God's approval, for to Samuel's human eyes, they all looked strong and eminently capable for the job, but one by one, God rejected them:

> Do not look on his appearance or on the height of his stature, because I have rejected him; for the LORD does not see as mortals see; they look on the outward appearance, but the LORD looks on the heart.
> (1 Samuel 16:7)

It's as if God looks for the star inside the scabby apple. He doesn't judge us by our wrinkled skin or blemishes, or our less-than-shiny appearance. Instead, God looks at the heart. He knows the gifts, character and opportunity invested into each person, because He gives them. And His divine gifts are what we all carry to enable us to reach our own 'star potential'.

Remember how the nuns sang about Maria when she was in the abbey? That she was a flibbertigibbet, a demon, even, and a problem? Nevertheless, Maria was to soon show her 'star quality' and grow in confidence to fulfil her potential.

Moments for musing

Accepting God knows our real potential, the hidden 'star' inside us, how might you discover that inside yourself?

Are there people you made snap judgements about, before learning how wrong you were?

What first impression do you project to others? How accurate might that be?

Do you carry any hidden prejudices that shape your first impressions about people who do not look or live like you?

Prayer

Dear Lord, help me to see other people as You do, and not be swayed by first impressions or external appearances. Amen.

16
Grace at the Table

After those less-than-favourable first impressions, Maria's first dinner with the family also fails to get off to the best of starts. She arrives rather late in the dining room as the family sit in silence, with plates of food going cold in front of them. It's not just their glasses of water that are chilled, the whole atmosphere is frosty. Yet Maria breezes in, seemingly unabashed, as the children watch her closely. She pulls out her chair to sit down, only to bounce back up with an undignified yell before removing a large prickly pinecone from her seat as the children stifle sniggers. Maria seems to have fallen foul of a practical joke set up by her new charges.

The family pick up their forks to start eating, yet Maria looks surprised because they have forgotten to say 'grace'. Wordlessly, everyone lays down their forks and Maria leads them in a prayer of thanksgiving for the meal. A stony silence hangs in the air; it appears that the von Trapp dinner table is not the place for relaxed banter or conversation. Unperturbed, Maria chatters on regardless as she begins to eat, and thanks the children for the precious gift they left in her pocket earlier. When asked by the captain what gift she is referring to, the children pause mid-mouthful and aghast. They are waiting for Maria to tell their father about their earlier prank of planting a toad in her pocket. The captain is losing patience, yet Maria continues blithely on, undeterred. Instead of getting the children into trouble, she explains with delightful disregard how this being her first day, they knew it was important for her to feel accepted, and had been so kind and thoughtful to welcome her. Of course, that was the exact opposite of the reality, as Maria and the children are all aware. The delightful scene unfolds as the more effusively Maria thanks them, the more the children look ashamed, until one by one the younger ones begin to sob. 'Oh, they're just happy,' Maria smiles to the bemused captain, as if it's all completely normal.

Maria started their meal by saying 'grace', a thank you prayer. Yet the word 'grace' is so much more than a pre-meal prayer. When the word 'grace' is used in the Bible, it refers to an undeserved gift that is freely given. It is displayed in how God showers love and forgiveness upon us, despite the fact that all too often we don't deserve it. You cannot earn grace, for grace depends on the goodness of the giver, not the merit of the receiver. The apostle Paul writes a lot about grace, including in this passage to the Ephesians:

> For by grace you have been saved through faith, and this is not your own doing; it is the gift of God – not the result of works, so that no one may boast. (Ephesians 2:8-9)

Along with the word 'grace' in the Bible, we often see the word 'mercy'; especially about God who is both 'merciful and gracious' (Exodus 34:6; Psalm 86:15; Psalm 103:8). These two characteristics complement each other. For as grace is *giving* someone what they do not deserve, mercy means *not giving* someone what they do deserve. Grace and mercy are divine characteristics, and aspects of God's character that we are also called to show and share with others.

Undoubtedly, the greatest act of grace was offered by Jesus on the cross, accompanied by His incredible statement of mercy towards those who crucified Him: 'Father, forgive them; for they do not know what they are doing' (Luke 23:34).

At that first family dinner in the von Trapp house with all those hidden tensions, Maria showed mercy by *not giving* the children the rebuke they deserved, and also showed grace by forgiving them for their unkind behaviour. Those characteristics of grace and mercy would soon endear her to her new charges and eventually to their father, although there would be a few metaphorical mountains to climb before that.

Moments for musing

How important is it for you to remember to thank God for His daily provision, especially before a meal, or when receiving other gifts and blessings?

When have you received an undeserved gift of grace that showed something of God's character?

How might you choose to offer grace and mercy when needed, especially when it is not so easy?

Prayer
Dear Lord, thank You for Your amazing grace. Help me to show grace and mercy to others as You show them to me. Amen.

17
Sixteen Going on Seventeen

During dinner, a telegram arrives for Captain von Trapp, and its arrival brings a smile to Liesl's face. For the arrival of a telegram means the arrival of the telegram boy. As she slips away from the table to greet her 'beau', Maria is astute, and notices Liesl's reaction.

Out in the garden, the young lovers are flirting by the gazebo. The telegram boy, Rolf, is self-confident and considers himself wise, a man of the world. I suspect Liesl, with her secret smile, is not as naïve as she pretends to be! It is a scene reminiscent of a more innocent era, when 'courting' had different rules and conventions. Yet, despite its anachronistic dialogue, this little scene introduces a song that has become a firm favourite ever since.

Liesl may well be humouring Rolf as she sings about needing someone older and wiser; someone who will tell her what to do. And while resisting any suggestion of acceptable condescension from Rolf, there is something important to grasp, for we all need people around us who can share their wisdom and experience. Learning from each other is how we work together in community. We look out for others, and learn to ask for and accept advice and help. Supporting each other is one way we strengthen relational bonds.

In the New Testament, we can read one of Paul's letters to his younger colleague, Titus. In this, he explains how different generations should teach and support each other and pass on the baton of faith (Titus 2:1-8). Paul is encouraging the teaching of faith between young and old, because it is not always our chronological age that matters, for we all have things to give and receive, regardless of age.

In recent years, the passions of a Swedish teenager, Greta Thunberg, have hit the headlines as she has openly challenged the international Establishment about the realities of climate change. She has been a young prophetic voice to challenge those in power, as well as the rest of us, to take seriously environmental issues. In 2014, Malala Yousafzai was a co-recipient of the Nobel Peace Prize and became the youngest-ever Nobel laureate. She was seventeen years old. Just two examples where age is no barrier to making a difference – whether that is old age or young age.

The apostle Paul wrote to another young protégé, Timothy, urging him not to be defensive of his youth when teaching others:

> Let no one despise your youth, but set the believers
> an example in speech and conduct, in love, in faith,
> in purity.
> (1 Timothy 4:12)

Paul knew his time on earth would be short, and that he needed to encourage the next generation to keep going and hold fast to God's message. He himself had been taught by the first believers, and was so inspired by their faith that he committed his life to do the same for the next generation. That deep conviction to pass on God's love and message gave us much of the New Testament that has inspired Christians across the world ever since.

Like Paul, wherever and however we live out our faith, we never do so in isolation. Unwittingly or otherwise, we will influence others by our words, actions and attitudes, so by being intentionally positive and cooperative, we can each make a difference, wherever we are.

Liesl sings that she will depend on Rolf, but as the plot unfolds, we see how he is influenced by the wrong ideology. Liesl cannot in the end depend on him, for as much as we need each other, people are fallible. Yet we are not left alone, for we have the infallible, dependable Holy Spirit to help us learn and grow, as Jesus promised the night before His crucifixion:

> I have said these things to you while I am still with you. But the Advocate, the Holy Spirit, whom the Father will send in my name, will teach you everything, and remind you of all that I have said to you. Peace I leave with you; my peace I give to you. I do not give to you as the world gives. Do not let your hearts be troubled, and do not let them be afraid.
> (John 14:25-27)

With that in mind, we can all echo something of Liesl's last line in that song: I will depend upon You, Lord!

Moments for musing

How have other people inspired and encouraged your walk of faith?

Who might you be able to encourage and inspire?

How could you learn to depend more on the Holy Spirit's infallible presence and guidance?

Prayer

Dear Lord, help me be a willing learner and teacher, to listen and learn from You and others around me. Amen.

18
I Shouldn't Be Telling You This, But...

It doesn't take long for Maria to unpack and settle into her new bedroom; there's not much to hang in the wardrobe. What a change in her surroundings the last twenty-four hours has brought. Last night, she was sleeping in a nun's 'cell', and tonight she is settling down in a palatial room in an affluent family house. As she makes herself at home, Frau Schmidt, the housekeeper, arrives, bearing reams of fabric for Maria to make new dresses and replace the shabby one she arrived in.

Frau Schmidt has been employed by the captain for many years. She remembers what life was like when his late wife was alive and the home was full of music and love. Now it seems that grief has wrapped its cold arms around the von Trapp family and the joy has vanished. The housekeeper has observed many a governess come and go before Maria, all unable to cope with the children. Maria, though, is optimistic about her new position, although there is more than a flicker of scepticism on Frau Schmidt's face.

Standing in the bedroom doorway, the housekeeper shares her own opinions of the captain's future plans. She leans in to Maria to whisper conspiratorially, admitting she shouldn't really be sharing her 'news' about the captain's plans to propose to the baroness.

'I shouldn't be saying this, but...' While it was tempting to share her 'insider knowledge', deep down Frau Schmidt knew it wasn't right to gossip. That's why she was looking over her shoulder to see if anyone was around to hear her.

Like Frau Schmidt, we too usually know when we should be keeping quiet. There might be that prickle of conscience, otherwise known as the Holy Spirit, whispering, 'Don't say it!' Yet sometimes we too cannot resist spilling the beans.

We could say that a gossiper is a person with a good sense of rumour. Rumours, like gossip, can undermine confidence and relationships. If they are correct and based on truth, then we have shared information that is not ours to share, and possibly better kept private. And if its 'false news', then we've undermined the truth about a person's character or situation. Sometimes it's as if our tongues have a mind of their own before our brain or our conscience clicks into gear.

Gossiping is not a new problem. Around AD60, James, the half-brother of Jesus, wrote a letter to the early Church. In it, he says the tongue is a small thing (in our body) that can set off a whole chain of events:

> With it we bless the Lord and Father, and with it we curse those who are made in the likeness of God. From the same mouth come blessing and cursing. (James 3:9-10)

It is wonderful to chatter freely with friends, to share news and thoughts, to ask about the welfare of others and show concern about those whom we can genuinely support. However, when we know that we 'shouldn't be telling you this', then it is definitely better not told!

We cannot be too hard on Frau Schmidt, because she's a character in the film who has been given a line to move along the unfolding plot. She helps us to know what is unfurling in the minds and lives of our characters. And, of course, if she was real, we couldn't judge her anyway, for as Jesus said, 'Let anyone among you who is without sin be the first to throw a stone at her' (John 8:7).

However, this snippet of film dialogue may prompt us to remember that words are rather like toothpaste squeezed from a tube – really easy to squeeze out but impossible to put back in.

Moments for musing

Why does that idea of taming the tongue resonate with us as humans?

If you hear others gossiping, might you join in, keep quiet or perhaps challenge the justice of the conversation?

How might you become more confident to 'gossip the gospel' – and willing to share in your everyday conversations the good news of Jesus and His love for us all?

When I was a child, I was told that 'sticks and stones can break your bones but words can never hurt you'. Do you agree with that?

How can we make our words healing and helpful to others and to ourselves?

Prayer

Dear Lord, help me to control my tongue so
that I become more fluent in encouragement
and speak words of love and life. Amen.

19
Maria Kneels to Pray

At the end of her first day in the von Trapp villa, Maria kneels by her bed to pray. It won't have been the first time she's done this, for abbey life was shaped by a rhythm of prayer, from early morning matins to evening compline. And now in her new bedroom, she's chatting with God as if with an old friend, freed from the liturgy of convent prayer.

Isn't that what prayer is? Talking freely with our loving God who has unlimited power, infinite awareness and knowledge, and is present at all times and in all places? God is King of all kings, so what an incredible privilege to talk with Him directly. He is more accessible than celebrities, presidents or earthly royalty. We don't need an invitation into His presence; we don't need a human mediator to speak to Him.

As Maria prays, she has a growing realisation that her new role has a purpose. Remembering Frau Schmidt's words, she begins to wonder if her role may include preparing the children for their new mother. We might smile at her assumption, for she is right, but not in the way she expects.

At different times and in different ways, we can all pray. Prayer has so many dimensions, from worship and thanksgiving to confession, to holding someone we care about before God. In prayer we are asking God to intervene, to help, to change things. Sometimes our prayer requests feel 'answered' relatively quickly; at other times they appear 'unanswered', or resolved in an unusual way. However, our prayers are never 'unanswered' because God has promised to hear us and to respond with all that is good, at the right time. Even if that is not in the way or the time we expect. As Jesus reminds us:

> For everyone who asks receives, and everyone who searches finds, and for everyone who knocks, the door will be opened. Is there anyone among you who, if your child asks for bread, will give a stone? Or if the child asks for a fish, will give a snake? If you then, who are evil, know how to give good gifts to your children, how much more will your Father in heaven give good things to those who ask him! (Matthew 7:8-11)

From our perspective, we cannot see ahead, or see the bigger picture, and we never have the eternal or universal view that God has. All we have is the longing, the yearning, the hoping and the desperation for a change in a situation, and that becomes the right impetus for our prayers.

While we cannot share God's eternal perspective, what we can do is trust that He sees all and knows all. When we pray, we are sharing our personal longings, yearnings and hopes and offering our petitions to the Holy One who has both the compassion and the power to make a difference.

In prayer, we are seeking God's kingdom's blessings for those who need help and hope; what an incredible privilege.

So, I shy away from the concept of a 'successful' prayer being an 'answered' prayer. Perhaps it's better to consider every prayer as a triumph of faith in itself. Prayer is the evidence that we, are asking and trusting God to intervene in the right way at the right time.

Several years ago, when exploring the idea of being ordained in the Church of England, I was asked about my prayer life. I admitted that, rather than a timetable of structured prayers each morning, God was more like a parrot on my shoulder. He was that little voice in my ear and close enough to hear my constant whisperings. I remember thinking afterwards; it may not have been the wisest thing to describe God as a parrot! Thankfully they saw through my clumsy explanation.

I later discovered a kindred spirit in Smith Wigglesworth, who was born in 1859 and considered one of the great British evangelists. He is quoted as saying, 'I never pray longer than half an hour. On the other hand, half an hour never passes without me praying.'[4]

I do try to prioritise a daily time of prayer with God – it recalibrates my thinking and is an intentional choice to keep Him first in my life. However, I couldn't just do one 'prayer time' then switch off for the rest of the day, because the whole of life is an opportunity to 'practise the

---

[4] There are multiple sources for this famous quote. See for example: www.prayermagazine.com/articles/a-life-given-oversmith-wigglesworth.php (accessed 30th December 2022).

presence' of God. And it is 'practise' in both senses of the word.

God is with me in everything, in my thinking and doing. My spoken prayers are a running commentary of emotions, desires, faith and praise, offering God all that I am and all that I have. I am not, however, the first person to understand that idea of what could be called 'practising the presence of God'. Nearly 400 years ago, a French monk called Brother Lawrence had that same idea, that a relationship with God goes beyond a 'quiet time'. Brother Lawrence made every moment a holy moment, whether that was in formal chapel services or when washing dishes or mending shoes. His understanding of living in this constant grace and presence of God is written in a book called *The Practice of the Presence of God*.[5]

Maria's life in the abbey had been shaped by prayer; prayer was like a bookend at the beginning and end of each day, and affected everything in between. Now she's got to discover and develop a new way of living outside the abbey walls. Becoming a governess will bring many more activities to prevent her from keeping up with her old routines. For many reasons, none of us can ever spend enough time with God. There is always so much to distract and occupy us; not just our tendencies to procrastinate or forget. So we may feel inspired to pray more, but any condemnation that we are not good enough is never from God. Even Paul the great apostle failed to get his life of faith right all the time, as his rather convoluted confession explains:

---

[5] Brother Lawrence, *The Practice of the Presence of God* (New Kensington, PA: Whitaker House, 1982).

I do not understand my own actions. For I do not do what I want, but I do the very thing I hate … For I know that nothing good dwells within me, that is, in my flesh. I can will what is right, but I cannot do it. For I do not do the good I want, but the evil I do not want is what I do.
(Romans 7:15,18-19)

Like Paul, I grapple with failed self-expectations. So I give myself permission to be fallibly human, and pray as I can, not as I can't. I relax and practise the presence of God, and develop a natural listening to Father God.

Moments for musing

When does a 'pondering' before God become a prayer – is there a difference?

How might you practise the presence of God?

Are there people who could help you develop a greater confidence in praying?

What passages in the Bible reassure you that God welcomes and hears our prayers?

Prayer
Lord God, help me to pray as I can, not as I can't. Help me to relish the time we spend together. Amen.

20
Praying and Playing

Having been given bolts of fabric to make new dresses, Maria asks Frau Schmidt for more fabric to make play clothes for the children. The housekeeper pronounces in reply that the von Trapp children march; they do not play. Maria is flummoxed; surely all children play? Apparently not in this household, where life is structured and days are filled with purpose but no play. Then, as she bids her goodnight, Frau Schmidt mentions that Maria's bedroom is due for some new curtains for her windows.

A little while later, there's a fierce thunderstorm that rattles the house and prompts the song 'My Favorite Things', with more on that in the next chapter. But before then, after the captain has burst in to break up the children's singing, Maria, ever the opportunist, seizes the moment to ask him about making play clothes for the children. His answer is an emphatic 'no'; such frivolity is unacceptable. His unyielding response infuriates Maria, although she appears to accept his decision. The captain asserts his authority by stating that despite his extended stay in Vienna, he expects Maria to live by his rules in his absence. No argument, no play clothes, no playing.

Struggling with the idea that playing is off limits, Maria sits discouraged and frustrated. Glancing at the metres of fabric draping her windows, she realises these soon-to-be discarded bedroom curtains are eminently recyclable. Perhaps she might not be so biddable after all...

However young or old we are, play is fundamental to our development and quality of life. We're designed to 'work, rest and play', as that old commercial for a well-known chocolate bar used to advocate. OK, we might not play with marbles or at dressing-up games as we did as children, but life is for living. We *are* created to release our inner child and delight in simple things, to discover life with its absurdities and quirks, and find the fun – to play!

Recreation that distracts and brings joy is as important for adults as children. Life has so much serious stuff to contend with that most of us need to be reminded to relax from time to time.

Someone asked me how my husband and I continue to get on so well, especially as we're together all day most days. 'Perhaps it's possibly because we pray and play together,' I offered. For me, 'play' might be doing something creative, like baking, crafting or playing a board game. My husband will walk the dog or serenade me (or the dog) from his remarkable memory bank of old songs. He's particularly keen on cycling freewheel downhill as the wind rushes past. For all of us, play releases endorphins and reduces stress; it helps us recalibrate and recreate who we truly are, so it is not surprising that the word 'recreation' reads as 're-creation'.

Jesus' teachings were life changing and challenging and often peppered with hyperbole and humour, from His image of a camel walking through the eye of a needle (see

Mark 10:25), to His first public miracle at a wedding after the wine ran out and He saved the day by transforming jars of water into gallons of wine. And not just cheap plonk either, but the very best wine (John 2:1-10). That is so much evidence that God delights in life in all its fullness and joy.

Jesus says He came that we 'may have life, and have it abundantly' (John 10:10). That abundance of life is promised for eternity, but eternity starts here and now. Abundance today is about finding the richness of life beyond the mundane. We know life isn't always a playground and there will be troubles, yet in those tough times He promises us the *joy* of His strength (see Nehemiah 8:10).

Joy is different from happiness; we can experience divine joy despite our circumstances. I remember being in hospital after my third miscarriage, and feeling desperately sad and hopeless. It was less than a month after becoming a Christian and I felt confused and alone despite being in the middle of a busy ward. Then another patient came by and asked if I was all right. I clearly wasn't. She was a Christian and responding to the Holy Spirit's prompting to leave her room and talk to me. She sat with me as I cried, and then offered to pray. As she prayed, despite my sadness I felt joy. It was rather bizarre and my first experience of the actual 'joy of the LORD' (Nehemiah 8:10), feeling the joy of God's presence and peace, which gave me strength in that moment.

Maria's joy for life is infectious; it might have been misplaced at times in the abbey, but as a governess she brings something priceless and precious. She resolves to make the children their new play clothes from her old bedroom curtains; to bring 'play' back into their lives; to help them remember the joy of living and loving. That sense of play is infectious and, before too long, Captain von Trapp himself will rediscover that same joy.

Moments for musing

How do you relax and 're-create' yourself?

Have you got your balance of work, rest and play about right?

How can you develop more intentional times to play and de-stress your life?

Prayer
Dear Lord, thank You that You came to bring abundant life. Help me relish moments of joy and play as I live and work. Amen.

21
My Favourite Things

After Maria's less than encouraging start as the new governess, she settles down for her first night's sleep. At this point, it is pouring with rain. As the storm gets worse, there are lightning flashes and thunder crashes, and Maria's bedroom door bursts open. One by one, the children arrive, seeking comfort from the storm. The younger girls dive under her quilt, while the boys pretend to be unfazed by the wild weather outside. With all the children around her, Maria tries to distract them and tells them that when anything bothers her or she feels unhappy, she thinks about different things, nice things, her favourite things.

And so begins one of the most optimistic songs ever written. Yet it's so true: when we feel sad, remembering and refocusing on our favourite things can make us feel so much better. Another way to consider our favourite things is to think of the many blessings we have. We might consider the word 'blessing' as recognising and remembering all good gifts given by God. Gifts that bring us joy, peace and provision.

Remember how Maria sang about those packages that are tied using string? Brown paper parcels can look very ordinary, but underneath the wrapping is the promise of excitement and surprise. I've come to realise that many of the best blessings may seem ordinary because they are so common. Yet being familiar doesn't stop them being really special, like the extraordinary blue of a clear sky, and the fact that I can actually see it. Or that I can hear the blackbird sing – which isn't a foregone conclusion for everyone. Or that I can get out of bed each morning, again not a foregone conclusion for everyone. Indeed, there was a time when my back was so bad I couldn't get out of bed. Then there's the blessing that I have a long list of friends' numbers to call upon. There are real, everyday blessings like hearing my grandchild's giggle, or my husband's daft old jokes. Sometimes we are surrounded by blessings but forget to notice them.

I've got another sign in my house; this one says 'Count Your Blessings'. It's a big sign because I need to be reminded often. It can be too easy to focus on the rubbish or mundane and take too much for granted. Doing that positive daily refocus does help me to feel better.

Whatever the circumstances, whatever the storm, there are always blessings – somewhere. And it's a choice to notice and recognise that which is positive. And if, when it's really tough and all we can thank God for is that we are not alone in the storm, well, that is a blessing too.

The apostle Paul knew many challenges, some of them listed in 2 Corinthians 4:8-11, yet despite all he experienced, he understood how to keep positive:

> Therefore, since we are justified by faith, we have peace with God through our Lord Jesus Christ, through whom we have obtained access to this

grace in which we stand; and we boast in our hope of sharing the glory of God. And not only that, but we also boast in our sufferings, knowing that suffering produces endurance, and endurance produces character, and character produces hope, and hope does not disappoint us, because God's love has been poured into our hearts through the Holy Spirit that has been given to us.
(Romans 5:1-5)

So next time, when the metaphorical insect stings, or when we're feeling low, let's remember Maria's song and our own favourite things. There will always be, somewhere, blessings so that we may refocus.

Moments for musing

How might you notice blessings, especially those that could be taken for granted? You could start a 'Joy Journal' in a notebook, or a 'Joy Jar' with little notes popped in a jar each day. These can be great to look back on and remember your own favourite things.

Where might you be a blessing to someone else? Blessings don't have to be onerous to make a difference.

How can we turn thankfulness into worship?

Prayer
Dear Lord, help me to always notice my blessings and to develop that 'attitude of gratitude' to lift my spirit no matter what's going on around me. Amen.

22
Global Warning

We don't know how long it is after the thunderstorm that Maria and the children emerge from the constraints of the house rules to play on the hills. It could be days or even weeks, and so much has already changed in them. Defying the captain's instructions, they are now wearing those infamous play clothes made from Maria's old bedroom curtains. The meadow is lush and green, giving them a stunning 'playground'. As they run and sit and sing and play, we're invited to remember what the world should look like. Fresh, pure, clean and a joy to share...

Sadly, though, we know that those commissioned to care for God's creation haven't always cherished it. And by 'those commissioned' I mean us; those of us who have lived in the last couple of hundred years of 'human progress' – all of us, to a greater or lesser extent.

Those movie scenes were filmed more than half a century ago, so who knows what those meadows look like now? Hopefully still beautiful, despite the fact that our world has become a more polluted and damaged environment. Perhaps those streams that trickled with mountain melt water aren't quite so crystal clear, or the fresh air that filled Maria's lungs isn't quite as fresh as it once was. Or, bringing that closer to home, we may notice fewer butterflies or birds in our neighbourhood, or see plastic bottles and fast-food wrappers strewn across grass verges.

When God made our world, humanity, the pinnacle of His creation, was commissioned to tend and nurture it, to be a good steward of the earth's resources, so the whole human race and creation could flourish together. With increasing impunity, we allowed greed and selfishness to push the boundaries of good stewardship up to, or even beyond, the point of sustainability. We face a disturbing prognosis over the health of our increasingly sick ecosystems. Who knows if, or when, we will reach the point of no return? The voices for change and action are loud, but are they loud enough?

Meanwhile it won't be us who actually bear the full impact of the unfolding damage. It will be the generations yet to come who will live with the catastrophic disappearances of essential flora, fauna and sustainable ecosystems. Then there is the real and increasing suffering of billions of people as a direct result of global warming. That was not God's original plan for our world or for humanity, as Genesis records:

> Then God said, 'Let us make humankind in our image, according to our likeness; and let them have dominion over the fish of the sea, and over the birds of the air, and over the cattle, and over all the wild animals of the earth, and over every creeping thing that creeps upon the earth.'
> So God created humankind in his image,
> in the image of God he created them;

male and female he created them.

God blessed them, and God said to them, 'Be fruitful and multiply, and fill the earth and subdue it; and have dominion over the fish of the sea and over the birds of the air and over every living thing that moves upon the earth.' God said, 'See, I have given you every plant yielding seed that is upon the face of all the earth, and every tree with seed in its fruit; you shall have them for food. And to every beast of the earth, and to every bird of the air, and to everything that creeps on the earth, everything that has the breath of life, I have given every green plant for food.' And it was so. God saw everything that he had made, and indeed, it was very good. (Genesis 1:26-31)

After such an auspicious beginning, the rest of the Bible unfolds to show that God is still working to restore us to our original purpose and relationship, which is to cherish and be cherished and to walk with Him and each other in peace; to fulfil our commission to nurture the beauty and bounty of His world and all within it.

Moments for musing

What realistic actions and decisions could you take to make a sustainable difference?

How could 'sustainability' be part of your Christian ethic and principles?

Could you consider championing your local church to take part in the A Rocha UK initiative, 'Eco-Church'?[6]

Prayer

Dear Lord, please help me recognise the health of our planet and the impact of my lifestyle.
Help me actively cherish Your creation.
Amen.

---

[6] For more information, see ecochurch.arocha.org.uk (accessed 8 March 2023).

23
Do-Re-Mi

Maria and the children are wearing their new clothes made out of old curtains. They sit in the meadow to sing, but to Maria's surprise, the children don't know any songs, for the von Trapp household has been devoid of music and joy. So Maria decides to teach them. She reaches for her guitar and begins to strum one of the most famous songs from the film. She introduces them to the basic musical scale, do-re-mi-fa-so-la-ti-do. They learn that it is the base to build every song.

Yet it's not just singing that starts this way; everything worth learning begins with the basics. So starting at the very beginning is a very wise approach. It is such a good idea that it is even in the Bible – twice!

'In the beginning' are the first words of the first chapter of the first book of the Bible. They introduce us to God who spoke life into nothing, then over time created a fully formed, finely tuned universe teeming with a spectacular array of life.

That account of the beginning was written down many, many centuries before any modern scientist understood cosmology or what has become known as the Big Bang theory. Yet that poetic prose in Genesis reflects much of our broader scientific understanding of the planet's development. Light and dark, water and land, seeds and plants, times and seasons, living creatures and, lastly, humanity.

So that is a good beginning. But there is another place in the Bible that also starts with the words 'In the beginning', and that's the Gospel of John. This Gospel opens with a kind of prequel to Genesis, as we discover the source of the voice that said, 'Let there be light' (Genesis 1:3).

After a lengthy Old Testament that has set the stage for the birth of Jesus, this second 'beginning' in the New Testament offers a new depth in our understanding of God:

> In the beginning was the Word, and the Word was with God, and the Word was God. He was in the beginning with God. All things came into being through him, and without him not one thing came into being. What has come into being in him was life, and the life was the light of all people. The light shines in the darkness, and the darkness did not overcome it.
> (John 1:1-5)

'In the beginning was the Word'... the 'Word' being the Author of life himself. The 'Word' is a proper noun because He is the person who had the power and creativity to speak life and light before even time itself began. John wrote that before everything, there was always God and has always been God. One God yet in three distinct persons: God the Father, God the Son and

God the Holy Spirit. It is a complicated idea to wrap our brains around.

Yet that shouldn't be too surprising, for we have human brains, and it needs a God-sized brain to grasp the intricacies of our Trinitarian God. One God in three persons? Each separate yet co-dependent and one Being? He is indeed unexplainable within our human vocabulary and so mysterious that we cannot actually quantify or put Him into any known category, and no analogy can actually reflect the whole truth.

However, we are not left in a total vacuum, for God knows that we need to see and experience something to help us understand it. We need our faith to be 'fleshed out', so to speak. We needed someone to show the way, to explain things, to be a living visual aid. And so, 2,000 years ago a baby was born. A unique baby, a once-in-all-of-creation baby, conceived by the miracle of God and born of a woman in Bethlehem.

Jesus might have had His mother's smile but He had His heavenly Father's divinity. A baby-sized foot, you might say, in both camps, both fully human and fully divine. This miracle birth didn't just appear out of the blue, but out of God's blueprint for all humanity, at just the right time and in just the right way.

Rather like Maria's musical building blocks that teach the children to sing, John's words are the building blocks that help shape Christian faith, the basic understanding of God – Father, Son and Holy Spirit; all three, but one. All very present, all fully God, distinct yet separate, one God, interactive, interdependent and very real for all time. Whole libraries have been written to explain this so I won't attempt to summarise 2,000 years of theology into anything more than; yep, it's real and it is a mystery!

When we start singing, we need to do something more with those few notes, do-re-mi, and not just stick to that one scale for every song! Maria teaches the children that when you know those notes to sing, you can then sing anything. I still find it quite incredible that every different song and melody is constructed from such a limited number of musical notes.

As a singer, Maria knew how to construct do-re-mi into so many glorious songs. And she didn't just know them theoretically; she also sang them, taught them, shared them and danced to them. They were part of who she was.

Jesus is like the composer of life who comes to sing alongside us. It is as if He came to teach us to join in the Father's love song. The very beginning of faith often starts, not with a 'do-re-mi', but a question: 'Is God real?' Then we delve deeper and discover God in all His complexities and wonders.

Moments for musing

Where in the Bible can you find passages that show God being one God yet in three distinct persons?

How do you relate to each Person of God, as Father, Son and Holy Spirit?

What were your own first steps of faith?

Prayer
Dear Lord, help me grow in my
understanding of You as my Trinitarian God.
Help me embrace every new beginning that I
have in You. Amen.

24
The Tools You Use

It took me years to realise I wasn't really supposed to be singing 'Dougha dear' and 'Raya drip of sun'. But even though I'd rather skewed the lines, I did love to belt them out from my stage atop the footstool to any willing audience. I was probably nine years old at the time...

That song stirs the soul of *The Sound of Music* aficionados and inspires the least musical of us to sing along. It captures the new joy in the children; they whizz around the lake on bikes, trot through Salzburg in a horse-drawn carriage and dance around the fountain in the Mirabell Gardens. When I visited Salzburg, I wasn't the only one recreating that scene, jumping up and down those now famous steps while my husband disowned me.

Maria explains how those few notes, do-re-mi, form the basis of every musical composition. She explains that they are the tools needed to build a song. Once you know them then you can sing a million (at least) different tunes.

Music needs building blocks, tools to create a song; but whatever we do, we invariably need specific tools to do it well. Yesterday I needed a bucket of them because I was in the garden tackling rampant overgrowth. I needed to weed and prune, cut back bedraggled roses and end-ofseason tomatoes. My job was made easier because I had a big bucket full of tools: a kneeling pad, trowel, plant food, secateurs, a narrow pointy 'thingy' to excavate deep-rooted weeds and thick pink gardening gloves. I could have knelt on the wet grass without the kneeling pad, or wrenched off roses without secateurs. I might have yanked out weeds less effectively, or done it gloveless and got all nettled or prickled. But everything in my bucket made gardening much easier and more productive.

So what about the tools that help us live a life of faith? What do we have in our 'spiritual bucket' to help? Whether we are new to faith or a seasoned Christian, God has given us spiritual tools to help and encourage us.

The primary tool is, I suggest, the Holy Spirit who is the power and presence of God Himself. Jesus said that after His final departure the disciples would not be left alone:

> I have said these things to you while I am still with you. But the Advocate, the Holy Spirit, whom the Father will send in my name, will teach you everything, and remind you of all that I have said to you.
> (John 14:25-26)

And He did come, some fifty days later at Pentecost, as a holy wind swirled and flames of fire alighted upon the waiting disciples. That event became the means for supernaturally empowering *all* God's people, not just a few chosen ones, which had been the case in Old Testament days. *All* people could now have direct access to God's presence as divine counsellor, enabler, encourager and truth-prompter.

Another powerful tool is the Word of God, Scripture. Words that are 'inspired by God' (2 Timothy 3:16) to equip us every day. Jesus used that Scripture tool Himself when faced with the devil in the wilderness; three times, Jesus used the truth of Scripture to dismiss the devil's snares:

> Jesus answered him, 'It is written, "One does not live by bread alone."' ... Jesus answered him, 'It is written,
>> "Worship the Lord your God,
>> and serve only him."'
>
> Then the devil took him to Jerusalem, and placed him on the pinnacle of the temple, saying to him, 'If you are the Son of God, throw yourself down from here, for it is written,
>> "He will command his angels concerning you,
>> to protect you ...
>> so that you will not dash your foot against a stone."'
>
> Jesus answered him, 'It is said, "Do not put the Lord your God to the test."'
> (Luke 4:4,8-12)

God's truth could quash the devil's temptations, because God's truth is stronger than lies or even half-lies. With scriptural gems like those available to us, the more we read Scripture, the more we are likely to find pertinent verses to help boost our faith. And because I don't have a photographic memory, I need another tool in my spiritual bucket – a concordance to help me locate a particular passage when I've forgotten where to find it!

Forgiveness is another tool, which is the equivalent of a spiritual weedkiller. Unforgiveness is rather like

Japanese knotweed invading a beautiful flowerbed; so forgiveness conquers such peace-invaders like guilt or resentment *before* they become deeply rooted. The 'rule for that tool' is because God has forgiven me, I can and will choose to forgive others. It is not always easy or immediate so it has to be a choice, as Paul wrote:

> As God's chosen ones, holy and beloved, clothe yourselves with compassion, kindness, humility, meekness, and patience. Bear with one another and, if anyone has a complaint against another, forgive each other; just as the Lord has forgiven you, so you also must forgive.
> (Colossians 3:12-13)

Then there is worship, which is like plant food for the soul to help us grow spiritually stronger and healthier; plus, of course, those incredible 'tools' of spiritual armour:

> Stand therefore, and fasten the belt of truth around your waist, and put on the breastplate of righteousness. As shoes for your feet put on whatever will make you ready to proclaim the gospel of peace. With all of these, take the shield of faith, with which you will be able to quench all the flaming arrows of the evil one. Take the helmet of salvation, and the sword of the Spirit, which is the word of God.
> (Ephesians 6:14-17)

With the promise of all those tools available for us at all times, we have access to every tool we need as His confident, beloved children.

Moments for musing

What tools do you rely on when doing practical jobs around the house?

What spiritual tools can you recognise, and how do you use them?

How might you use the image of spiritual armour to encourage and equip you day to day?

How might you encourage someone else to make more use of the spiritual tools God has given?

Prayer
Dear Lord, please help me recognise the spiritual tools I have and use them more effectively, so I may walk in Your freedom and love. Amen.

25
Me, A Name I Call Myself

Fräulein Maria was making real headway with the von Trapp children. Her first job on meeting the children had been to learn seven names (and untangle a few spurious ones along the way, when they tricked her with incorrect names). Unlike her unpopular predecessors, Maria's name soon became a byword for fun and acceptance, a name that would one day evolve into 'Mother', but don't let that plot spoiler be too distracting for now...

As Fräulein Maria teaches her new charges to sing 'DoRe-Mi', one of the lines she sings is quite profound. It's the line that speaks of 'mi' being the name we call ourselves. If we tweak the spelling of that little word from 'mi' to 'me', then it offers something wonderful to reflect upon.

Our world spins around each 'me' on the planet. I remember quite clearly as a child, that moment when I understood I wasn't the centre of the whole world. I was very young, but there was a definite revelation that other people were a 'me' as well. It was, I guess, a turning point in my emotional maturity. I wonder if Jesus had that moment when He was growing up in Nazareth – when He became aware that He lived in a whole world of people

115

who were all entitled to call themselves 'me'? Or was He already aware of that, with His divine brain in a child's body? Some questions will just have to wait until we meet Him face to face.

God introduced Himself to some of the earliest men and women of faith as 'I AM'. This account of Moses' conversation with God at the burning bush recounts when He revealed His name for the first time:

> But Moses said to God, 'If I come to the Israelites and say to them, "The God of your ancestors has sent me to you", and they ask me, "What is his name?" what shall I say to them?' God said to Moses, 'I AM WHO I AM.' He said further, 'Thus you shall say to the Israelites, "I AM has sent me to you."' God also said to Moses, 'Thus you shall say to the Israelites, "The LORD, the God of your ancestors, the God of Abraham, the God of Isaac, and the God of Jacob, has sent me to you":
>
> This is my name for ever,
> and this my title for all generations.'
> (Exodus 3:13-15)

That self-identification by God implies that He is the ultimate 'me' of all 'mes', the one and only 'I AM'. No other name or title is needed or necessary. 'I AM' identifies Him as the beginning and the end of all creation. He was bigger than any single name could describe; He was God of all and about to rescue His people from slavery in Egypt. He had, in fairness, already gathered various titles from His people that spoke of His character and power. Yet within all of those titles, He gave Himself just one name: 'I AM.' It was enigmatic for sure, but recognising that His holy name is rooted in the verb 'to be' is encouraging, for out of God's *being* comes His *doing*. In every place, past, present and future, God just *is*.

And while He is the First Person in everything, He chose to step out of that eternal being to become a human being. When Mary was looking for a name for her baby, she didn't have to consult any name books or follow the family traditions, because angel told her, 'Do not be afraid, Mary, for you have found favour with God. And now, you will conceive in your womb and bear a son, and you will name him Jesus. (Luke 1:30-31). Jesus' God-given name would shape His purpose and actions. 'Jesus' being the Greek variant of the Hebrew name 'Yeshua', or 'Joshua'. It means 'the Lord saves'.

When Jesus grew up and started His public messianic ministry aged around thirty, He would sometimes refer to Himself by that same ancient divine name of 'I AM'. Here are seven examples from John's Gospel, moments when He overtly linked Himself to the person of God – 'I am the bread of life' (John 6:35), 'I am the light of the world' (John 8:12), 'I am the gate for the sheep' (John 10:7), 'I am the good shepherd' (John 10:11), 'I am the resurrection and the life' (John 11:25), 'I am the way, and the truth, and the life' (John 14:6), 'I am the true vine' (John 15:1).

Whenever Jesus used that name, 'I AM', of Himself, it caused a massive commotion (John 8:58-59) for to even utter the holy name of God was deemed a blasphemous assault on everything holy and proper. Unless, of course, the person using that holy, unsayable name was actually God! The lack of understanding that Jesus was truly God, wasn't limited to the Pharisees and their peers; it was a challenging concept for everyone, and still is today.

Jesus knew who He was. His identity was sure and steadfast and shaped every action and word. When we grasp who Jesus is, it helps us grasp who we are too. Jesus promised that *His Father* becomes *our Father* through faith, which is something we remember every time we say the Lord's Prayer.[7] No longer am I just Bryony, the vicar/writer, for that is my job title. No longer am I Bryony, mum, grandma, sister, wife, friend or daughter, for they are my relationships. I am Bryony, child of God and daughter of the King of kings... that is who I am, and rightly truly significant in God's eyes.

Each one of us is an individual 'me' for whom Jesus came. We are each a unique 'me', and together we make up a world of individual 'mes'. Each one of us is wonderfully precious to the great 'I AM'. Me is quite a magnificent name!

Moments for musing

Who are you?

Reading through the I AM statements of Jesus in John's Gospel, how might they help develop a deeper understanding of who Jesus is?

Prayer
Dear Lord, because You are the great 'I AM', I can be fully me. Help me grow in the confidence of being unique and loved within Your eternal family. Amen.

---

[7] Matthew 6:9-13.

26
The Captain Returns

After the exuberance of 'Do-Re-Mi', there is a hiatus between songs as we catch up with Captain von Trapp. In this next scene, he is driving back to the villa with his two close friends, Baroness Elsa von Schraeder and Max Detweiler. Drawing close to home, they drive past a bunch of noisy children hiding high in the trees that border the road. The captain dismisses them as local urchins, before doing a mental double take. Surely not... you can almost see that thought flit across his brain... surely they cannot be his children?

Once back home, we see the palatial grounds of the von Trapp villa in all their glory. And having stayed at the film's location, Schloss Leopoldskron, outside Salzburg, I can confirm it is beautiful, even though when I visited the weather was unseasonably grim.

The captain and the baroness stroll through the grounds, with the spectacular mountains reflected in the lake, as the baroness asks how he can leave such a beautiful place. His reply is rather sad, as he confesses to pretending to be madly active, for activity suggests a life filled with purpose.

Here is a man seemingly with everything, in the prime of life, with health, wealth and a luxurious home filled with servants and children. He is a respected naval commander with a glittering career and the resources to do exactly what he wants; yet he lacks purpose and fulfilment. Money cannot buy happiness, even if it allows us to be miserable in comfort.

In Matthew's Gospel (19:16-26), there's an account of another rich man who was seeking fulfilment. He came to ask Jesus what he should do to inherit eternal life. He seemed to be seeking something beyond earthly wealth; searching for that elusive contentment money cannot buy. Jesus, who loved and knew him, understood it was his wealth that had bound him up. He had made an idol, a god, out of his riches.

Now, there is nothing wrong with being rich or successful, or having power and prestige and a glittering career. But when they become the driving force for life, then God can become a secondary priority. It's not money that's the problem, it's the 'love of money', as the writer to the Hebrews wrote:

> Keep your lives free from the love of money, and be content with what you have; for he has said, 'I will never leave you or forsake you.'
> (Hebrews 13:5)

It can be really hard to suggest to people who seem to have everything that they might need the one thing money can't buy. When everything that seems worth having costs so much, it is hard to accept that the greatest gift is free of charge. And for anyone who lives by the maxim, 'There is no such thing as a free lunch,' then the free gift of God's love can be too much to accept.

As a human race, we are all looking for fulfilment. It's as if we have a God-shaped hole in our core being. It can feel easier to try to fill that hole with other 'stuff'; to ease the emptiness with human affirmation, wealth, power and prestige, or numb the yearning with an unhealthy appetite for material things or passing stimulants.

I remember being in my early twenties and searching for meaning and identity. I decided the answer was to train to be a beautician and make a successful business for myself. But it didn't work out. Not that there is anything wrong at all with being a beautician! It was just the wrong answer for me in that situation. Years later I realised that deep yearning had been the Holy Spirit calling. I had been yearning, not for something but for Someone, and had sought meaning in the wrong way. Yet God never gives up, and ten years later I found the completion, peace and identity that I had yearned for, when I discovered that Jesus was real and relevant and vital to my whole life.

God is not coy or difficult to find; He's only a whispered prayer away. The captain tells the baroness that he is searching for a reason to stay, to be settled. That searching is rooted in us all until we find our deepest fulfilment. The question is, will we recognise it and follow it to the heart of God himself?

Moments for musing

What makes you feel fulfilled and gives life purpose? How do your choices reflect that?

What might you say to friends or family who are asking what 'life in all its fullness' (John 10:10, GNT)? might mean for them?

Can you identify ever feeling that God-shaped hole?

Prayer

Dear Lord, help me to find You as the One who offers all purpose and meaning in life. Help me avoid seeking fulfilment in the wrong places. Amen.

27
You're My Saviour

As Captain Georg von Trapp and Baroness Elsa wander round the garden, she is fishing for confirmation that he's as keen on her as she is on him. Thanks to some canny script writing, he takes the bait and tells her she is lovely, charming, witty and gracious and a perfect hostess. Then he says, 'and in a way, my saviour'. To which Elsa laughs because that doesn't sound quite so romantic. Georg replies softly that she is the one who has brought meaning back into his life.

'You're my saviour!' is a common phrase, and one I've used when someone brings me a much-needed cuppa, or we might say it to the mechanic who rescues us and our broken-down car. A saviour is someone who saves us, and it's not just a religious idea.

Last summer I was trying to rescue a honeybee from the house by attempting to coax it outside to safety. It had been trapped for a while and was clearly flagging. If I'd let it 'bee' (forgive the pun) it would probably have died. So I was being kind and attempting to help that frustrating buzzing creature, but did it recognise my help? Clearly not! It resisted every attempt to coax it into my 'bee-spoke' insect catching beaker to take it outside. I wished I could speak 'Bee' to reassure I meant no harm, and was just being friendly and helpful.

Saviours come in all guises; some with cups of tea, some with spanners, some with a beaker and cardboard lid. Some are literal lifesavers, some less vital, but nonetheless appreciated. Georg von Trapp has found hope of romance in Elsa von Schraeder, although she admits that under all her glamour and glitz, she is really just as lost as him.

All through Old Testament times, the people of God cried out for a Saviour. They had been oppressed by invading armies, were prey to their own sin and had experienced natural and human disasters. After generations of longing, their promised freedom seemed no nearer. They wanted someone to swoop in and save them, to make it all right. Someone big enough, brave enough and powerful enough, with a mighty army to conquer every enemy. What they hadn't fully grasped was that the biggest enemy they faced was not an external one like an invading enemy, but one within themselves.

They knew a Saviour would come because God had promised. Then, after centuries of believing and hoping, a carpenter in Nazareth claimed He was the Saviour they had been waiting for. On one particular Sabbath in the Nazareth synagogue, Jesus summarised His role as the One to set God's people free:

> He stood up to read, and the scroll of the prophet Isaiah was given to him. He unrolled the scroll and found the place where it was written:
> 'The Spirit of the Lord is upon me,
> because he has anointed me

to bring good news to the poor.
He has sent me to proclaim release to the
    captives
and recovery of sight to the blind,
to let the oppressed go free,
to proclaim the year of the Lord's favour.'

And he rolled up the scroll, gave it back to the attendant, and sat down. The eyes of all in the synagogue were fixed on him. Then he began to say to them, 'Today this scripture has been fulfilled in your hearing.'

(Luke 4:16-21)

That extraordinary announcement in the synagogue should have been greeted with universal joy and relief. Instead, He was mocked, derided and dismissed. Saviours, it seems, don't always look like we expect. They wanted a knight in shining armour but they needed the equivalent of a heart surgeon. They wanted a powerful general with an army, or another Moses with plagues to smite the enemy, yet they got a teacher without an army. They got God, born to walk among them, able to speak their language and tell them He was offering to free them from captivity.

Milton Jones in his brilliant little book *10 Second Sermons* expresses what it means to 'be saved': 'Salvation is like being returned to factory settings. But you have to admit there is a factory and there could be some settings.'[8]

The 'factory settings' of God's original plan include how we were designed to live in a full, free and loving

---

[8] Milton Jones, *10 Second Sermons* (Darton, Longman & Todd, 2011), p22.

relationship with Him. But because the human race rebelled against both the 'factory' and its 'settings', we allowed a yawning chasm to separate us from God. He abhors this chasm even more than we might, so He made a plan to bridge that chasm in person and restore us to our 'factory settings'.

He stretched out His arms on the cross to bridge the chasm between God and His people. Imagine, one bloodied, nail-punctured hand reaching into the heart of heaven, as the other hand reaches into the heart of every person who ever lived, to draw each one of us into God's love. Only God was able to touch both heaven and humanity at the same time. Only God both recognised the problem and then became the solution.

Humanity has always needed saving from both harm and armies, but more than that, we need saving from ourselves. That is why we need a spiritual and eternal Saviour. Through Jesus, we don't just become Christians who might go to church and become very, very nice; we become *fully human* in a *fully restored* relationship with God.

Moments for musing

What did you, do you, need saving from?

What does it feel like to know that Jesus is our absolute eternal Saviour?

Why not read the earthly life story of Jesus as written in one of the Gospels? Notice how people related to him and what He said about salvation.

Prayer

*Dear Lord, please help me recognise and
receive Your saving love, and fill me with
confidence that I am forever Yours. Amen.*

28
You Really Must Learn to Love Yourself

On the terrace, Elsa and Georg are chatting as Max Detweiler is munching apple strudel; perhaps he's unhappy, Georg suggests? Max admits he's frustrated because he's lost the singing group he wanted to book for the forthcoming Salzburg Festival. After a brief chat, the captain walks away, but not before he throws in an insightful observation, as Max tucks into his third slice of strudel, that Max must really must learn to love himself.

I understand that need to console myself or celebrate with food! In emotional and stressful situations, eating can be less about 'need and nutrition' and more about comfort. I know I'm not alone. We eat to live, but we also eat socially, emotionally and habitually – and, unfortunately, for some it can become a real problem. A third slice of strudel won't solve Max's problems. The captain's insight is wise, for if Max learns to love himself, then he'll discover something precious to carry him through every challenge.

Loving ourselves is something we are invited to do by Jesus. One day He was being tested by cynical religious leaders who wanted to catch him out:

> One of them, a lawyer, asked him a question to test him. 'Teacher, which commandment in the law is the greatest?' He said to him, '"You shall love the Lord your God with all your heart, and with all your soul, and with all your mind." This is the greatest and first commandment. And a second is like it: 'You shall love your neighbour as yourself.' On these two commandments hang all the law and the prophets.'
> (Matthew 22:35-40)

Jesus had simplified their myriad religious laws into: love God first and foremost, love each other and love yourself. Although that seems short and simple enough, it's not always that easy! Learning to love ourselves is a lifetime challenge because rather than accepting and cherishing all that is good in us, we often focus on what is lacking. We know what's in our heart and mind and, if we're honest, we don't always like ourselves.

It may be, too, that we consider loving ourselves as self-indulgent or prideful. But that is not what Jesus is prompting us to believe. Too often we show other people the kindness, grace and forgiveness that we deny ourselves. And unlike God, who is infinitely kind and patient, we can be our own sharpest critic and judge. Yet God really does know us, right down to the murkiest core of our being.

Years ago I didn't particularly like or love who I was. However that sad verdict had evolved, it was an indication of the shame and blame I carried. That lack of love for my inner 'me' was crippling, causing false assumptions about relationships and my place in the world. Since then, I have learned to accept God's unconditional love and, although I'm really, definitely not perfect, I am loved; and apparently quite likeable, to most folk, anyway!

One way to learn to love ourselves starts with recognising who God is. The more we recognise who He is, the more we trust that His Word is true. His Word says we are made 'in his image' (Genesis 1:27), and surely anyone made in God's likeness will be pretty amazing?

Or perhaps we think that loving ourselves is big-headed? We surely cannot consider Jesus to be 'big-headed'! He simply accepted the truth that He was beloved by Father God. So when we look afresh at what divine love is, then we can understand how truly loving our own self isn't arrogant or misplaced.

Paul's remarkable explanation of love explains how God loves us so that we can share that with other people. But it also reminds us how to love ourselves:

> Love is patient; love is kind; love is not envious or boastful or arrogant or rude. It does not insist on its own way; it is not irritable or resentful; it does not rejoice in wrongdoing, but rejoices in the truth. It bears all things, believes all things, hopes all things, endures all things.
> (1 Corinthians 13:4-7)

One day I trust that I shall meet God face to face and see His face shining with the love He has for me. Meanwhile, the process of learning to love ourselves may take a while, possibly with the odd slice of apple strudel along the way. It might involve forgiving ourselves; being patient with ourselves. It might mean giving ourselves time and permission to be as kind, persevering and gentle to ourselves as we are with others.

Moments for musing

What barriers prevent you from grasping how much God loves you?

What can you begin to do to cherish yourself as God Himself cherishes you?

What are the top five positive, encouraging things that others might say about you? Asking a close friend why they are your friend may give you some clues!

Prayer
Dear Lord, please help me understand how much You love me. Help me to love and like myself too. Amen.

29
You Must Help It

This next snippet of our film only takes a few seconds, yet carries a message that's as relevant now as it's always been. We enter the scene as a young lad cycles through the villa gardens and stops beneath a large tree. It is the telegram boy, Rolf, who danced with Liesl in the gazebo. He dismounts from his bike to chuck pebbles at what we presume to be Liesl's bedroom window in a clumsy attempt to attract her attention. He doesn't get far before being interrupted by the captain, who demands to know what he's doing.

The boy turns, flustered, and desperately tries to formulate the right answer. Suddenly, though, he collects himself and, standing tall, clips his heals to attention. He raises his right arm in a salute and barks out 'Heil Hitler!' shedding youthful discomfort for determined confidence.

That salute infuriates the captain. His expression could be enough to make the boy turn and run, but Rolf walks towards him and hands over a telegram for Herr Max Detweiler. Now he has carried out his errand, the captain sends the boy packing. Rolf's political leanings are clearly unwelcomed.

As the boy cycles away, the baroness walks up to Georg and murmurs that he is just a boy, to which Georg retorts that he is just an Austrian. Max rather unwisely pipes up that whatever is going to happen will happen, so make sure it doesn't happen to you. The captain turns on him angrily and tells him to never say that again. Max's rather passive response is to explain that while he has no political convictions, he can't help other people's. That is enough to infuriate Georg even more, and he tells Max that he can help it; indeed, he *must* help it

As Max walks away somewhat nonplussed, Georg leans over the balustrade next to the baroness, and sighs. He is an experienced military man and knows only too well that his country is on a political knife edge. The political manoeuvrings of 1930s Germany are already impacting their lives. It is time to stand up for what he believes in; however personally, socially or professionally awkward that will become.

The captain's words remind me of the quote, 'The only thing necessary for the triumph of evil is for good men to do nothing.'[9]

'Turning a blind eye' and apathy are indeed collaborators of evil intent and injustice. Throughout every age, our world has witnessed power struggles and battles on every level, from the schoolyard bully to the despotic dictator trapping innocents in their wake of destruction.

We live now in different times from those of Maria, Max and Georg, yet we still face destructive conflicts, immense human suffering and challenges across the

[9] Often attributed to Edmund Burke (1729-97).

world. Now, as when this film was set, those who fail to condone such actions are, to some extent, complicit in the face of injustice. Perhaps it's useful to reflect on the difference between the concepts of 'turning a blind eye' and 'turning the other cheek'. Meanwhile, the fight for freedom and justice will continue until the 'Prince of Peace', Jesus (see Isaiah 9:6), returns. Until then, we are challenged to speak up for those who are persecuted, to speak truth to power when necessary:

> Give justice to the weak and the orphan;
> maintain the right of the lowly and the destitute.
> Rescue the weak and the needy;
> deliver them from the hand of the wicked.
> (Psalm 82:3-4)

The people of God are called to be the hands of God. To reach out to those who lack the resources to help themselves. We are called to be the voice of God and to inspire justice. We are called to model the character of God and stand up for righteousness. And with all of that, wherever we walk, we are called to take the gospel of peace:

> Stand therefore, and fasten the belt of truth around your waist, and put on the breastplate of righteousness. As shoes for your feet put on whatever will make you ready to proclaim the gospel of peace.
> (Ephesians 6:14-15)

People will always hold different opinions and values rom ours; that is the nature of community. But unlike Max's determination to keep quiet, and possibly compromise his integrity to avoid trouble, the captain's heartfelt plea is that we all must care, and that goes to the heart of the Christian gospel.

Moments for musing

What causes and situations tug at your heart, and how do you respond?

How might you recognise when and where there is injustice?

How could you become an agent for change and work to bring freedom for those who are oppressed? What stops you?

Prayer
Lord God, help me notice when and where I can make a difference and be bold enough to do what I can, in Your name. Amen.

30
The Turning Point

Every good story has a turning point. Think of any film you've seen and chances are there'll be a turning point almost always prompted by some kind of crisis. In films and fiction, that usually points towards the inevitable happy ending, and in this next scene we see the turning point in *The Sound of Music*.

After his confrontation with Max, prompted by Rolf's Hitler salute, we now see the softer side of Georg. He has set aside his boatswain's whistle and is relaxed and flirting with the baroness, setting the scene for an imminent proposal of marriage. However, breaking into their romantic moment by the lake comes the distant sound of squealing and giggles. They look to see a small rowing boat, and in this boat Maria and the children are obviously having great fun. Upon spotting the captain, now unexpectedly home, they attempt to stand and wave enthusiastically at him. Which is an interesting manoeuvre because boats of that size are not designed for eight people to suddenly stand up in! So it's not surprising that as they wave and yell, the boat capsizes and Maria and the children tumble into the, fortunately shallow, lake.

Georg is most definitely *not* amused, although the baroness, standing behind him, clearly is. She stifles a chuckle while understanding this is not supposed to be funny. In the melee that follows, the children help each other out of the water and Maria grabs the boat to tow it to shore. The children emerge from the lake, drenched, laughing and thrilled to see their father.

In that instant, the gentle man we have just witnessed reverts to the stern patriarch. He commands them to stand in line, blowing that whistle again to call them to attention. Every laugh dies on the lips of his sodden but safe family. The baroness makes a discreet exit as the children are ordered to get dry and change into their uniforms.

Then it's just the two of them, a dripping Maria standing face to face with the captain. He's holding his daughter's sopping headscarf and hesitates, before demanding of Maria if he has just seen his children actually climbing trees? Have they been running around Salzburg dressed in old curtains? Her affirmative answers compound his fury.

Standing firm, Maria pleads the case for these precious children to play and relax. She wants him to know how much they love their father, even if they fear him too. She implores him to understand the different needs of each child, all desperate for his love and attention. But the more she tries to explain, the more he shouts her down. Their argument can only end one way and, not unexpectedly, he orders her to pack her bags and leave. He will not be told by anyone how to raise his children, and certainly not by a passionate young nun he expected to be meek and obedient.

This is a tense scene illustrating two kinds of anger. Looking objectively, we would probably sympathise with Maria and applaud her passionate outburst. She has recognised how much the children need their father and yearn to engage with him. She's grown to love them and wants the best for them. We could reflect that her anger reflects God's righteous anger at the injustice and pain of their situation. It's an anger that won't stay silent in the face of something wrong, as illustrated when Jesus overturned the money lenders' tables in the temple:

> Then they came to Jerusalem. And he entered the temple and began to drive out those who were selling and those who were buying in the temple, and he overturned the tables of the money-changers and the seats of those who sold doves; and he would not allow anyone to carry anything through the temple. He was teaching and saying, 'Is it not written,
>
> > "My house shall be called a house of prayer for all the nations"?
> >
> > But you have made it a den of robbers.'
>
> (Mark 11:15-17)

Jesus was right to be angry, His anger was therefore righteous. This was no meek, mild Jesus; this was someone who wouldn't stay silent in the face of injustice and wrongdoing. The trading He saw in the temple desecrated this holy place. It reduced it from being somewhere where everyone was welcomed to worship, to a dishonest marketplace. The people coming to worship needed to purchase their intended sacrifices, but before they could, they had to change their regular currency for the elite temple currency. Yet instead of this being an honest deal, the system had allowed exorbitant exchange rates. Such unscrupulous dealing denigrated genuine worship and turned the temple into a fiscal goldmine. The temple leaders that so frequently opposed Jesus did nothing to stop it, and possibly even took a cut of the profits.

There are times when we are all called to challenge a corrupt system or call out prejudice or unethical practices, and yes, that might mean giving passion to our words, as Maria does that day.

Georg, however, is very angry. His seems less like righteous anger as he reacts to her honesty and those uncomfortable truths. While he would be relieved the children have not come to any harm after their soaking, I suspect his anger is more about the loss of family dignity and control. My husband reminds me that our sense of injustice is strongest when we secretly know the other is right. It can be hard (as I have experienced) to hear uncomfortable truths, and we can become quite vehement in repudiating them!

This scene presents us with a challenge. What drives our own anger, our frustrations? When we 'see red', are we feeling a godly, righteous anger to do something positive, or are we reacting out of defensiveness, self-pity or bad temper?

As Maria and the captain continue to glare at each other, a sweet sound breaks into the heightened tension. It's the sound of music; charming, melodious singing coming from inside the house. Georg looks confused and asks Maria what it is. She tells him it's the children, singing the song she taught them to sing for the baroness.

They both go inside the house; the children are now dressed in their uniforms, wet hair combed and tidy (although how they got dried and changed so quickly is a mystery!). Liesl is playing the guitar as they all sing 'The Hills Are Alive with the Sound of Music' to a delighted Elsa and Max. Their beautifully harmonised interpretation of the song softens Georg's heart. He joins in and it all ends in laughter and an awkward but heartfelt hug between father and children. Maria smiles, watching from a distance, then turns to go and pack her bags. It seems that the sound of music has brought the harmony and healing she has been hoping for.

Noticing Maria leave, the captain excuses himself and follows her. His previous brusque manner now totally evaporated, he apologises to her, accepting he has behaved badly. He accepts that he doesn't know his children. Maria accepts his apology and responds with her own acknowledgement that her outburst was also inappropriate. He tells her he wants her to stay, then corrects himself and rephrases it more softly, as a request. Georg is already learning that demanding things is unhelpful. With a new respect between them, Maria offers to do whatever is necessary to help. Georg assures her that she has indeed helped, more than she probably realises.

In such difficult situations, someone has to reach out first to bridge the gap. It's not always easy, but that first offer of conciliation is worth its weight in gold. Knowing when and how to apologise, as Georg did, is a lesson we all need to learn. That, paired with Maria's acceptance and her admission that she too was out of line, brought healing to their relationship. It takes two to argue and two to make up.

Turning points like this scene are often moments when those involved start to see the other person more clearly. It is as if blinkers are removed and things become clear; as if they recognise there is a person involved, not just a problem to be sorted.

There was a vital turning point in God's eternal story when, 2,000 years ago, Jesus was born. During the three years He spent with His disciples, those close to Him each had their own personal turning point when they recognised who He was. This is the moment when the proverbial penny finally dropped for Peter:

> Jesus went on with his disciples to the villages of Caesarea Philippi; and on the way he asked his disciples, 'Who do people say that I am?' And they answered him, 'John the Baptist; and others, Elijah; and still others, one of the prophets.' He asked them, 'But who do you say that I am?' Peter answered him, 'You are the Messiah.' And he sternly ordered them not to tell anyone about him.
> (Mark 8:27-30)

Those who followed Jesus had already glimpsed something astonishing about Him. They'd witnessed miracles, seen Him close up and understood He was no phony. He seemed the 'real deal' – but as what? Who was this enigmatic man? In response to Jesus' seemingly simple question, 'Who do you say I am?', Peter's personal revelation articulated the turning point in God's eternal story: 'You are the Messiah.' That turning point for Peter, his epiphany, his *eureka* moment, shaped the rest of his own life and faith.

It takes God to reveal God; God working through His Holy Spirit to reveal Himself. And He does so in a way that connects our heart, mind and spirit to His truth. I believe God offers multiple opportunities for us to encounter Him until we, like Peter, suddenly recognise the person, the Holy Person, is the 'real deal', Jesus, God with us (see Matthew 1:23).

This turning point in Maria and Georg's relationship will reshape the whole family. It is our first glimpse of the unexpressed love between them, the love that Elsa notices rather too clearly; but that is for another chapter...

Moments for musing

What have been the turning points in your life?

Think about the conflict between Maria and Georg. Can you think of times when you have felt righteously angry about something and channelled that to make a positive difference somehow?

Thinking about times we experience unrighteous anger, ours or someone else's, how easy is it to offer and receive forgiveness?

Prayer

Dear Lord, help me to understand the difference between righteous and unrighteous anger, and to respond appropriately. Amen.

31
The Lonely Goatherd

After that previous turbulent scene when the captain and Maria clashed, this next scene is pure joy. The captain has softened and they are all beginning to relax into a new relationship. Maria and the children perform a puppet show for the delight of the captain, Elsa and Max. And so we are introduced to the lonely goatherd, although it has to be said, this is no ordinary little puppet show!

As Marta pulls backdrops and Gretl pushes props behind the 'stage', Maria and the older children sing and control the puppets from above. The figures of the lonely goatherd, the girl in the pale pink coat and her gleaming mama, wiggle and jiggle to the pull of strings. All that puppetry raises a question about how much we are controlled by God. Are we like puppets controlled by invisible, divine strings, with every move and decision already decided?

The answer to that question lies, I suggest, within the unconditional aspects of God's love. If, as we believe, His ultimate desire is for a relationship based on love, then that love has to be both freely given and freely received. Love that is demanded is not true love. Our choice to love Him, or not, stems from our free will to choose. God could 'pre-programme' us, but His motivation for wanting a genuine loving relationship is greater than His desire to control us.

Also, we know that God invites us to work with Him to help bring about His kingdom. If everything were totally preordained with Him as 'puppet master', there would be no need to pray, but pray we do:

> Do not worry about anything, but in everything by prayer and supplication with thanksgiving let your requests be made known to God. And the peace of God, which surpasses all understanding, will guard your hearts and your minds in Christ Jesus.
> (Philippians 4:6-7)

Years ago, I struggled to get up on dark mornings and get myself and the kids ready for school. Not being a morning person, I prayed for help. Miraculously, the next day, I awoke, unprompted, an hour earlier than usual. With unusual energy and zest, I bounded out of bed to get organised and avoid the usual morning chaos. Over the next few days this kept happening, until day four, when the novelty began to dwindle. I lay in my warm bed at 6.30am struggling with the idea of getting up. In that moment I felt God whisper, 'I might be able to wake you up but you actually need to get up!' So many prayers involve a partnership between us and God. We might pray but we also have free will to act.

Each day we make many thousands of decisions, big and small. Some are good and some not so good. Sometimes it's a simple decision, Choice A versus Choice B; but most of the time decisions are less binary. I don't believe God expects us to seek Him on every minute decision or action, like, 'What flavour ice cream shall I buy?' He's given us wisdom and experience to make our own decisions, because we have free will. He's given us common sense, too, and life experience and friends. And when we make a metaphorical 'pig's ear' of something, He has a knack of making it into a 'silk purse'. Or as Paul once wrote:

> We know that all things work together for good for those who love God, who are called according to his purpose.
> (Romans 8:28)

So while that puppet show in *The Sound of Music* is pure joy, it's not an analogy for the way God controls us. A better image to consider is the cheering and applause of Georg, Max and Elsa as they watch the performance; mirroring God's joy as He watches us learning to live in the fullness of His love. For in our relationship with God, there are, quite simply, no strings attached.

Moments for musing

Where in the Bible can you see accounts of people praying for God to intervene, and how did that change things?

We tend to feel safer when we have an element of control in situations. But how easy is it to share or relinquish control to other people when necessary? When might that be an important thing to do – and when not?

How might a desire to keep control affect your relationship with God?

Prayer
Dear Lord, thank You for the gift of free will.
Help me to use it well and find your best
purposes in my life. Amen.

32
Edelweiss

For such a little song, 'Edelweiss' carries a big story. It isn't – as I used to believe – the national song of Austria, or an ancient folk song. It was written purely for *The Sound of Music*, and apparently the last song Oscar Hammerstein wrote before he died, just nine months after the opening of *The Sound of Music* on Broadway.

It's a song about a flower; a small and fairly insignificant alpine flower that now adorns so much in Austria; from necklaces and bags to the Austrian two-cent euro coin. As a flower, though, it traditionally symbolised courage, bravery and love. If your partner brought you edelweiss, it meant they were so smitten that they'd ventured high into the mountains to gather them as a token of their love.

In the film, this song symbolises much about courage, bravery and love. We first hear it sung by Captain von Trapp, who has been locked in grief since his wife died. 'Edelweiss' is the song that helps him rediscover the love of his family and of singing. As he strums and sings, Liesl harmonises his melody; it is a tangible image of the harmony that now envelops the family.

For me, edelweiss has always been significant; when I was a child, my grandparents bought me an edelweiss necklace, knowing how much I enjoyed the film. I still have it; it's a reminder of my grandparents' love. The song will always be emotive, too, for it was the track of my childhood, filling the cultural gap between nursery rhymes and pop songs. I almost wore a groove in my vinyl record of *The Sound of Music*, not least because it was the only record I owned! When I became a mum, I sang it to my children at bedtime; then my daughter adopted it as her children's lullaby. I guess, sometime in the future, they may sing it to their own babies. So you can understand why this little nondescript flower is symbolic of much that I treasure.

Symbols are important; they help us relate the intangible to the tangible. In the Church, things that carry a special meaning, a holy meaning, are called sacraments. They're outward and visible signs of something invisible, mysterious yet very real to those who believe, like the holy mysteries of baptism or Holy Communion.

On the night before He died, at the Last Supper, Jesus took a goblet of wine and a piece of unleavened bread and shared it with His friends. He explained these were symbols of His blood that was about to be shed, and His body that was about to be broken. Ever since, Christians have shared Holy Communion as a reminder of that first Easter and His promise to return again:

> While they were eating, he took a loaf of bread, and after blessing it he broke it, gave it to them, and said, 'Take; this is my body.' Then he took a cup, and after giving thanks he gave it to them, and all of

them drank from it. He said to them, 'This is my blood of the covenant, which is poured out for many. Truly I tell you, I will never again drink of the fruit of the vine until that day when I drink it new in the kingdom of God.'
(Mark 14:22-25)

The bread and wine of Communion are symbolic. We don't really drink blood or eat actual human flesh! This is a sacramental meal, helping us remember the incredible, unseen gift of God's love, grace and mercy. We might recall its other name is 'the Eucharist', which stems from the Greek word for 'thank you', *efharisto*. Symbols really can mean so much.

Later, as the film reaches its dramatic conclusion, the von Trapp family sing at the Salzburg music festival. As the family come to the end of their performance, Captain von Trapp sings 'Edelweiss' as his finale. He knows that he and Maria will be attempting to flee with the children, over the mountains, but before they leave the stage, this last song symbolises his love for the Austria he sees as fading under Nazi subjugation. Perhaps, too, it is a cry for bravery and courage.

Despite being such a short and simple song, it has come to be one of the most recognisable tunes in popular culture. I wonder, then, if edelweiss can represent a gentle reminder that when we are brave enough to seek God's love, we will find something incredibly real?

May you know the love of God that can bloom and grow forever.

Moments for musing

What symbols help you engage with the wonder, love and grace of God?

What songs or traditions might you pass on to the next generations?

What tokens or treasures do you have that remind you of precious times or people?

Prayer

Dear Lord, please help me to spot those small things around me that speak of Your love and glory. Amen.

33
A Grand and Glorious Party

Baroness von Schraeder is an astute lady. She has already spotted the telltale signs of unspoken love between Georg and Maria. Elsa needs to 'bag her man', so she moves in swiftly to suggest that Georg throws a 'grand and glorious party' to introduce her to all his friends.

The promised party is indeed a grand and glorious event. The von Trapps' once neglected Golden Ballroom is the one we glimpsed when Maria first arrived. It is now glittering with chandeliers and tiaras as honoured guests dance to the music of an orchestra.

A stream of carriages draws up to the villa's entrance and the captain and baroness greet their guests. It's not long, though, before we see a hint of those pre-war political tensions. Such undercurrents will shortly surface, fuelled not least by Georg's Austrian flag on show in defiance of local and wider politics. Tonight, the von Trapp family and guests dance away their troubles.

As guests swirl and twirl to the music in the ballroom, the entranced children stand outside on the terrace peering through the doors. Liesl wanders off, dreaming of dancing with her imaginary 'beau'. She curtseys and begins a wistful, solitary waltz around the terrace.

Maria walks onto the terrace and joins the children as they share this magical moment. Just then, the music changes pace and the orchestra strikes up a new dance. Maria tells the children it's an Austrian folk dance called the 'Laendler'. Kurt wants to learn it so she takes his hands and shows him, counting one two three, one two three, step together, step hop… Halfway through their dance, amid a tangle of arms, the captain, who has also joined them on the terrace, walks up behind Maria and steps in to take his son's place.

The mood of the scene changes; the children appear to melt away and we see the chemistry between the captain and Maria as they dance around the terrace. They move gracefully and coyly, eyes locked on to one another. In wonderful cinematic kitsch, the camera shot becomes appropriately misty as Maria looks into the handsome captain's eyes, and then they pause… And with a sharp intake of breath she moves away, hesitant and embarrassed.

The baroness, however, has noticed, and steps out of the shadows to break the spell. Maria excuses herself, saying she cannot remember any more of the dance and Elsa reclaims her man, leaving Maria and the children to scamper off and prepare their surprise farewell song.

The romance in this film is touching, yet such romantic moments are not confined to cinemas. Some couples will tell of their own memories, when they realised there was a chemistry, a spark of love too delicious to be ignored. For others it may be have been love at first sight when eyes locked across a crowded room, or a slow-growing friendship that developed into something more. Every new relationship, every love story, will have its own journey. And for other people, like those nuns, their love might well be met within a relationship with God alone and supported by human friendship.

And so it is with our story of faith. The variety of ways couples meet and develop a relationship is reflected in the variety of ways believers explain how they came to faith. For some it is a dramatic conversion, even if less dramatic than Saul had on the road to Damascus. Saul was on a mission to destroy the early Church and was on his way to Damascus to quell the ridiculous notion about Jesus being the Messiah. While travelling, he encountered the risen Jesus (Acts 9:1-9). His story became an astonishing testimony of conversion, for Saul became Paul and the most prolific of apostolic writers and teachers.

Others may tell how they were raised in a Christian family, and steeped in Scripture and prayer before they could even talk. Those early foundations gave them all they needed to commit to their own faith. Their faith journey may have no identifiable moment of 'conversion', although their miracle is, I suggest, that they stayed rooted in that inherited faith and then claimed it as their own. Paul reminds Timothy about the power of his family's example of faith:

> I am reminded of your sincere faith, a faith that lived first in your grandmother Lois and your mother Eunice and now, I am sure, lives in you. For this reason I remind you to rekindle the gift of God that is within you through the laying on of my hands; for God did not give us a spirit of cowardice, but rather a spirit of power and of love and of self-discipline.
> (2 Timothy 1:5-7)

Many others in churches are like me, knowing a before and after of 'becoming a Christian'. There was definitely a time before I understood or accepted God's love, although I do remember how my life was peppered with many godly encounters and prompts to occasionally pray or go to a church. Most of those prompts revolved around remembering Maria and her calling to serve God. I wanted her surety of faith and belonging to something bigger, and quite fancied running across the hills wearing a dress made of old curtains – ever the romantic!

Those early hankerings of faith were significantly influenced by reading old family books about saints, especially Joan of Arc, and *The Sound of Music* (God works in mysterious ways!). My final decision, aged thirty, to accept Jesus as my own Lord was less theatrical than Saul/Paul's experience, but nonetheless life-changing.[10]

When we grow in faith, our relationship with God reflects how we grow in human relationships. Love, whether human or divine, begins with a first encounter, when we become intrigued and want to know more about the person. We may ask friends and family what they know about the one who has captured our heart. We will want to spend time with our new love and talk *to* them, and no doubt *about* them to anyone who will listen.

We know it is not always a straightforward and predictable journey. Peter, that wonderfully human example of Jesus' first disciples, knew what it was to fail and then be overwhelmingly forgiven and commissioned by Jesus. He begins his second letter with these words:

---

[10] You can read more about my experiences of discovering God's love on my website: www.bryonywood.co.uk.

Simeon Peter, a servant and apostle of Jesus Christ,

To those who have received a faith as precious as ours through the righteousness of our God and Saviour Jesus Christ:

May grace and peace be yours in abundance in the knowledge of God and of Jesus our Lord.
(2 Peter 1:1-2)

In that scene at the grand and glorious party, we glimpse something intimate and precious growing between Maria and Georg. However, whenever our journey of faith begins, there is a divine invitation to the greatest and grandest and most glorious party of all – when we will see the look of love on God's face as He looks at us.

Moments for musing

Thinking back over your journey of faith, what parallels are there in your experiences of human love – whether that's romantic love or a friend/family kind of love?

How much are faith and love entwined in all our relationships?

Who might you be able to encourage by sharing how you came to faith?

Prayer

Dear Lord, please show me how I might invest and grow in my relationships with the people I love. Amen.

34
So Long, Farewell

The captain has thrown that grand and glorious party and introduced the baroness to his friends. After that rather awkward moment between the captain and Maria, it is now time for the children to leave the party and go to bed. Ever the inspiring governess, Maria has taught the children a special goodnight song.

The guests gather in the splendid hallway to listen to the children sing a beautifully choreographed performance of sibling harmony.

What always puzzled me when I was younger was, why did all the children go to bed at the same time? It didn't seem right to me. My younger brother and I battled endlessly to assert fairness in our bedtimes. I was older so surely deserved to stay up later? It's a familiar battle, I suspect, in most families. Yet in the von Trapp household, not only was it not to be the night for Liesl's first glass of champagne, but she also appears to go to bed at the same time as sleepy little five-year-old Gretl.

Life isn't always fair, and some people seem to catch more than their fair share of troubles while others sail through life without major traumas. Some always land on their feet while others end up headlong in the mire.

Jesus told a story about some workers in a vineyard (Matthew 20:1-16). In that parable they were all paid the same, regardless of how long they actually worked. It seems to contradict the concept of a fair and just God. Jesus wasn't explaining industrial law; He was explaining God's law and how everything we receive is by God's grace, and not dependent on our own efforts or merit.

His audience would have been astounded. Was Jesus really suggesting that tax collectors, fishermen, 'loose women' and scruffy outcasts were as valued in God's kingdom as the religious elite or the great patriarchs, like Abraham and Moses? That very idea would have been scandalous to all who considered themselves pious and good.

Instead of being grossly unfair, though, God's offer of inclusive, unconditional love is the ultimate act of divine fairness. His kingdom has all kinds of topsy-turvy values, where the last is first (see Matthew 19:30) and all are equal. There never was, or will be, any heavenly hierarchy or pecking order. The keys to God's kingdom are faith and grace, not how worthy or good we are.

One place where this 'equal access policy' was seen was just outside Jerusalem at the 'Place of The Skull':

> One of the criminals who were hanged there kept deriding him and saying, 'Are you not the Messiah? Save yourself and us!' But the other rebuked him, saying, 'Do you not fear God, since you are under the same sentence of condemnation? And we indeed have been condemned justly, for we are getting what we deserve for our deeds, but this man has done nothing wrong.' Then he said, 'Jesus,

remember me when you come into your kingdom.'
He replied, 'Truly I tell you, today you will be with
me in Paradise.'
(Luke 23:39-43)

In His last earthly moments of human and divine agony,
Jesus demonstrated God's unending grace. That last-
minute confession of faith was enough to ensure the dying
criminal's place in God's kingdom. His 'ticket to paradise'
was just as valid as those who had believed and served
God their whole lives. Whether we consider it fair or not,
God loves us all equally; pauper or princess, archbishop
or archvillain. It is outrageous, of course, but then, God's
grace is outrageous.

A final thought: this 'farewell' song uses words we say
most days but rarely think about. 'Goodbye' is a shortened
version of an old English phrase 'God be wi' ye', a heartfelt
blessing upon departure. Also 'farewell' means just that –
'fare-well', proceed well, prosper as you go... Those
words of departure are laden with deeper meaning, even
if we don't always acknowledge it. A stroppy 'goodbye'
perhaps with a slammed door indicates the very opposite
of the blessing the word intends! Perhaps if we were to
think more about what we are saying as we leave, then it
might be easier to leave more graciously at times – like
Liesl did that night!

Moments for musing

How might you consciously wish God's blessings upon those you leave?

How might you avoid hasty or angry goodbyes?

Life is sometimes very unfair. How do you respond to circumstances that challenge your belief in God's love and fairness?

Prayer

Dear Lord, help me to treat others with the equality, generosity and fairness with which You treat me. Amen.

35
The Baroness 'Helps' Maria

After the grand and glorious evening, it's not just the children or the guests who leave the party. Someone else slips out unnoticed.

The children's song delighted the party guests and Max urges Georg that Maria be allowed to join the party. The look on the baroness's face suggests she is less keen to have this particular governess present for any longer than necessary. And although Maria protests at Max's invitation, she is persuaded and goes upstairs to change into 'something suitable'.

Baroness Elsa follows her and offers to help. She starts rifling through Maria's limited wardrobe, asking where that dress is that she wore the other evening when, she suggests, the captain couldn't keep his eyes off her. Maria looks aghast; the very idea of such an impropriety shocks her to the core. Elsa tells Maria not to pretend women don't know when a man is noticing, and they are both women. Well, they might both be female, but these two women couldn't be less alike in their understanding of worldly matters!

Elsa is rich and glamorous, a society lady determined to marry her man and affirm her place among the elite.

Maria has lived a sheltered life, embracing chastity, poverty and obedience and seeking to respond to God's love and serve Him as a nun.

It's a fascinating exchange; the baroness appears to be rather more manipulative than Maria realises. Elsa is certainly a woman of the world and used to getting her own way. So, when naïve but alarmingly attractive Maria potentially spoils her romance, well, that must be stopped. The baroness is speaking in honeyed tones, but with calculated effect. She has noticed once too often how the captain is distracted by Maria's innocent love and finds her beguiling. Elsa needs to clear her pitch. Now, I may be doing her a disservice, but watch Elsa's expression in those scenes with Maria and see what you think.

Elsa's warning and words have their desired impact. With steely resolve, she tells a horrified Maria that she must have noticed the way he looked into her eyes, for she blushed when they were dancing. The truth is too real for Maria to dismiss and she decides to leave at once, stuffing clothes into her battered carpetbag.

Elsa makes no attempt to change Maria's mind and promises not to tell anyone why she has run away. Satisfied with the result of her 'helping', the baroness swishes out of the bedroom in a rustle of haute couture satin.

Downstairs, as the orchestra continues to play at the party, we watch Maria as she places an envelope on the hall table before slipping out of the front door. She leaves as she arrived, dressed in her original 'the poor didn't want this one' dress and battered hat, with her guitar in hand.

There's an account in the Bible (Genesis 37–50) about Joseph. His older brothers detest their younger brother because he's the family 'golden boy'. Joseph seems to have an uncanny gift for prophetic dreams which hint at his future rise to power. His brothers initiate a malicious plot to kill Joseph; however, at the last moment they change their plan and seize the opportunity to sell him to passing slave traders.

Those rotten brothers return home to tell their heartbroken father lies about Joseph's death by a wild animal. Yet their brother is very much alive. Many years pass and, despite a very long and unjust prison sentence, there is an extraordinary family reunion. Joseph hasn't just survived his capture; he has eventually thrived. He has become Pharaoh's right-hand man in Egypt. Unaware of who he is, the eleven brothers eventually come before Joseph to beg for food and mercy, fulfilling those childhood dreams. Despite his brothers' wicked plan, it is God's good plan that works out in the end:

> God sent me before you to preserve for you a remnant on earth, and to keep alive for you many survivors. So it was not you who sent me here, but God; he has made me a father to Pharaoh, and lord of all his house and ruler over all the land of Egypt. (Genesis 45:7-8)

Detours and disasters may beset us, but they need not lead to ultimate despair and hopelessness. Nothing is wasted in God's eternal economy. In faith we can be sure that whatever proverbial spanners we or other people might throw, He is able to work it out for our eternal good:

We know that all things work together for good for those who love God, who are called according to his purpose.
(Romans 8:28)

The fourteenth-century English mystic Mother Julian of Norwich put it another way: 'All shall be well and all shall be well, all manner of thing shall be well.'[11]

The baroness intended to remove Maria from the scene, yet by sending Maria back to the abbey, she is giving her the space and time to pray…

Moments for musing

How might you be encouraged by the account of Joseph's life?

Can you look back to see how God has worked something for good in your life?

Who can you encourage while they struggle though a tough time?

Prayer
Dear Lord, so often I can't see Your hand in the events that unfold around me. Help me to trust that in all things You do and will work for good. Amen.

---

[11] www.norfolkwomeninhistory.com/1300-1499/julian-of-norwich (accessed 20 December 2022).

36
Intermission

Maria has dressed in her old convent clothes and is preparing to leave the villa before anyone notices. She walks through the empty hall and places an envelope on the table as the music rises to a crescendo of 'Edelweiss'. Then, with bag and guitar in hand, she walks to the front door, looking back wistfully before leaving and closing the door behind her. It is an emotive moment that leaves us hanging and waiting for a solution.

The screen goes black and the word 'Intermission' appears, giving us a moment to draw breath and return to reality. *The Sound of Music* is a long film, so this break was probably welcomed by all sitting spellbound in their cinema seats! This intermission is an integral part of the film's pace: Maria arrives... Maria leaves... and (without spoiling the plot too much) Maria returns...

It's a pattern echoed in the account of Jesus' life and ministry. He arrives... He leaves... and He returns. And now, 2,000 years later, we are living in what could be called the intermission of God's epic story.

Jesus has always been alive and real, as John's opening words in his Gospel remind us: 'In the beginning was the

Word, and the Word was with God, and the Word was God. He was in the beginning with God' (John 1:1-2).

So while there never was a time when Jesus was not actually real or alive, there was one particular moment when He stepped out of eternity to live among us on earth; He physically 'arrived'. But then, following His death, resurrection and ascension, He physically 'left', and what a sight that must have been, as Luke describes:

> So when they [the disciples and Jesus] had come together, they asked him, 'Lord, is this the time when you will restore the kingdom to Israel?' He replied, 'It is not for you to know the times or periods that the Father has set by his own authority. But you will receive power when the Holy Spirit has come upon you; and you will be my witnesses in Jerusalem, in all Judea and Samaria, and to the ends of the earth.' When he had said this, as they were watching, he was lifted up, and a cloud took him out of their sight. While he was going and they were gazing up towards heaven, suddenly two men in white robes stood by them. They said, 'Men of Galilee, why do you stand looking up towards heaven? This Jesus, who has been taken up from you into heaven, will come in the same way as you saw him go into heaven.'
> (Acts 1:6-11)

And just one look at today's news reminds us that while Jesus came to inaugurate God's kingdom, we are living in the 'now but not yet' of that fulfilled kingdom – the spiritual 'intermission' between Act One and Act Two as we wait for Jesus' return. We are between the first mission of God and the concluding mission of God – we live in the *inter-mission*.

We know *The Sound of Music* will continue after the intermission because intermissions are not at the end; the story is not finished. Maria still has to work out what God's call is for her life.

Like Maria, Jesus has a beloved family to rescue and lead to freedom and safety. This promised completion of God's kingdom is prophesied in the penultimate chapter of the Bible:

> 'See, the home of God is among mortals.
> He will dwell with them;
> they will be his peoples,
> and God himself will be with them;
> he will wipe every tear from their eyes.
> Death will be no more;
> mourning and crying and pain will be no more,
> for the first things have passed away.'
> … 'See, I am making all things new.' Also he said, 'Write this, for these words are trustworthy and true.' Then he said to me, 'It is done! I am the Alpha and the Omega, the beginning and the end.'
> (Revelation 21:3-6)

There will be a day when Jesus will say, 'It is done!' and He will once again dwell with us. What started in that Genesis garden will be completed in the New Jerusalem of Revelation. Yet even that won't actually be *The End*, rather the next Beginning, with a whole new way of living in God's completed kingdom, forever!

Moments for musing

How do you feel about the idea that Jesus will return one day?

No one knows when that day will be, so can we prepare for it and be ready to greet the return of the King?

What do books and movies with apocalyptic or Armageddon storylines show about the end of the world as we know it? How do they relate to biblical ideas of the 'end times'?

Prayer

Dear Lord, help me to serve and share Your kingdom values while I live in expectation of Your return one day. Amen.

37
Live the Life You Were Born to Live

The second half of the film starts with the children playing a very half-hearted ball game with the baroness. She is way out of her comfort zone as prospective stepmother, and suggests they continue the game tomorrow before escaping to sit with Max and drink pink lemonade.

Looking dejected, the children discuss Maria's sudden departure and decide to do something about it. They walk to Nonnburg Abbey and plead with Sister Margaretta to see Fräulein Maria, bewailing that she didn't even say goodbye. But it's no use; Maria is in seclusion and won't see anyone. The children are sympathetically but firmly ushered out as the iron gate clangs behind them.

Sister Margaretta ignores their protestations and walks away to talk with Reverend Mother. They are both concerned about Maria, who returned unexpectedly and without explanation. Sister Margaretta tells Reverend Mother that Maria isn't saying anything except in prayer.

The abbess decides it is time to discover what happened, so Maria is ushered into the study, looking very subdued. She explains that she left because she was frightened and confused. She returned because she knew it would be safe. The Reverend Mother responds by telling her the abbey can't be used as an escape from life.

Maria is insistent that she is ready to take her vows, but the wiser, older nun knows that would be premature in her current turmoil. She affirms Maria by telling her she has a great capacity to love, but her challenge is to find out how God wants her to spend that love... She then says something rather insightful: 'You have to live the life you were born to live.'

How do we know what life we were born to live? How do we know how to spend the love that lives inside us? These are two massive questions that probably shape more of our actions and reactions, decisions and emotions than anything else.

The Bible gives us one answer, which is that we are created with a great capacity to love because we are made in God's image. And His capacity to love is endless. We are so much more than flesh and blood; we are body, soul and spirit. So as much as we need to fulfil physical needs like water, food and shelter to survive, we also need a purpose in life and a network of relationships where we can both nurture and be nurtured. We are created to *belong* and know that we matter – to love and be loved. The fulfilment of physical needs will help us *survive*, but to *thrive* we need an understanding that we are significant somehow and to someone.

Discovering that through God we are secure, accepted and beloved is the greatest foundation for all human potential, the rock on which we can build our lives and the path to fulfilment and completion. There's a little verse within Psalm 37 that speaks about this:

> Take delight in the LORD,
> and he will give you the desires of your heart.
> (Psalm 37:4)

… although this isn't a prescription to manipulate God to do what we want, as in, 'Hey, Lord, I love You, so please help me win the lottery.' Nor is it a magic wand to ensure success, wealth or health. However, when we live enfolded in the *heart* of God, then we live in the *will* of God and are more in tune with the *mind* of God. When we 'delight in the LORD', our deepest human desires become attuned to God's desires. What we seek and hope for reflects the life we were born to live, with Him.

I remember a few years ago being at a glitzy Christian women's event; the glamorous speaker was sassy, funny and beautiful. I watched, feeling dowdy and grumpy, yearning to be like her. To be honest, I was envious; she seemed to have it all. Then that 'still small voice'[12] whispered, 'She has to run her race and you are to run your race.' I saw a picture in my mind's eye, one of those oval running racetracks with competitors running in different lanes. As long as they stuck to their own lane all was fine, but if they tried to cross into someone else's lane, or take a shortcut, then they collided and ended up in a messy heap.

Of course, it's great to be inspired and motivated by other people, but not to the extent of being envious of someone else's gifts and successes. I came away from that conference understanding that God was urging me to run in my own lane, discover my own path, discover my own

---

[12] 1 Kings 19:12, KJV.

gifts and ministry and learn to live the life *I* was called to live.

As a child, Maria heard the nuns singing and watched them working in the abbey. She wanted to be like them, yet it is becoming clear her life is about to take a different path. Not a lesser one, but different. As Reverend Mother reminds her, loving another person doesn't mean you love God less. For Maria to discover her purpose, she has to begin by facing the uncomfortable questions back at the von Trapp house. All she can do is take it one step at a time, and live the life she was born to live.

Moments for musing

How do you know when you delight in the Lord?

What *are* the desires of your heart?

What inner longings or dreams may be glimpses of 'the life you were born to live'?

Is what you do and how you live now reflective of your younger dreams and ideas?

Prayer

*Dear Lord, please help me to delight in You
and discover the desires of my heart. Amen.*

38
Climb Every Mountain

When I was a child, I would lift my record player's arm to skip this next song, 'Climb Every Mountain', on my *Sound of Music* LP. It just felt too dirge-y and boring after the exuberance of songs like 'My Favorite Things' and 'Do-Re-Mi'. At that young age, I was immune to the power the song carried or how pertinent the lyrics were to life's real challenges.

But with age comes experience, and, like the variety of songs in this film, we experience life in all its varieties and ups and downs. There are moments of pure joy and also struggles we wish we could skip over, like a song track. But the reality is that struggles have to be gone *through*, mountains have to be climbed and streams crossed, whether we like it or not.

Far from being boring, this song carries real depth. Perhaps Reverend Mother is not just singing it for Maria, but to remind herself that if something is worth the goal, it is worth the journey. She sings that however tough it is, every day of life becomes part of a journey to follow and find our dreams.

There is a lot in this song about mountains and rainbows, as there is in the Bible. And although they are beautiful images, biblical rainbows and mountaintops rarely indicate comfortable times. It was having struggled up the highest of mountains that people like Noah, Moses, Abraham and Jesus discovered that God was with them every step. The journey was hard but the view was worth it.

Rainbows, too, are used today in many different contexts; they are truly one of nature's most dazzling marvels. Those sweeping multicoloured arches as sunbeams and raindrops decorate our skies are glorious reminders that there is sunshine amid the storm. The Bible contains so many promises that no matter what happens, the Maker of the mountains and hills will be with us:

> Your steadfast love, O LORD, extends to the
>   heavens,
> your faithfulness to the clouds.
> Your righteousness is like the mighty mountains,
> your judgements are like the great deep;
> you save humans and animals alike, O LORD.
> How precious is your steadfast love, O God!
> All people may take refuge in the shadow of your
>   wings …
> For with you is the fountain of life;
> in your light we see light.
> (Psalm 36:5-7,9)

Habakkuk was an Old Testament prophet who understood what it was to trust God even when everything looked bleak:

> Yet I will rejoice in the LORD;
> I will exult in the God of my salvation.

GOD, the Lord, is my strength;
he makes my feet like the feet of a deer,
and makes me tread upon the heights.
(Habakkuk 3:18-19)

Maria sat in that study listening to Reverend Mother's song knowing she had to return to the von Trapps – all of them. She couldn't run away, but needed to face her troubles and climb her mountain of questions. One day, she would discover how to give all the love that she had and find her dream.

Moments for musing

What are the mountains and rainbows in your life?

Is there something you need to face, but may have been avoiding?

Rainbows remind us that there is sunshine amid the rain. How might that idea sustain you when life feels stormy?

Prayer
*Dear Lord, help me to climb the mountains of
my life, and give me strength for the journey
when the climb gets hard. Amen.*

39
Maria Returns

We don't know how long Maria stayed in the abbey praying through her turmoil, but it was long enough for the children to miss her. Long enough, too, for the captain and the baroness to become engaged. Meanwhile, the children are a dejected bunch. Yet, however dejected they feel, they are so different from those unhappy, uniformed, marching children who greeted Maria's initial arrival.

Now they are moping in the garden, united in confusion and melancholy, trying to remember the song Maria taught them. Their mournful, half-hearted rendition of 'My Favorite Things' doesn't lift their spirits at all. That is, until another voice, a familiar voice joins in their song.

Looking around, they spot Maria walking towards them and dash to give her overjoyed hugs, laughing their welcome. And it's not just the children who have changed. Maria too is very different from the gauche young girl who first arrived at the von Trapp villa. She is poised and confident, somehow beautifully dressed, although how and where did she acquire such a chic wardrobe?

Maria has thrown off that earlier flibbertigibbet image and has embraced Reverend Mother's challenge to see if there is any future in her love for Captain von Trapp. Almost immediately, the children answer that unspoken question to pop her bubble when they blurt out that their father and the baroness are to be married. As if on cue, the captain himself appears. Again, he's a very different character from the whistle-blowing, cold disciplinarian we first met.

Life changes us, people change us, God changes us. Those changes tend to happen slowly, almost imperceptibly, although I've noticed it's usually in my toughest times that I end up learning the most! Good times, easy times seem to have less effect on character formation. And as much as we are totally beloved by God, we have much to learn as we continue to grow into His character. It takes a teachable spirit and a degree of humility to allow God to help us become the best we can be. It takes a whole lifetime, and only in hindsight do we recognise how much we've matured and grown in character and faith.

What really strikes me in this scene is the unconditional welcome around Maria's return. Despite their confusion at her sudden departure, the children harbour no grudge and embrace her wholeheartedly. The captain, too, merely mentions that she left without saying goodbye; it is a simple question without implied criticism. Only the baroness looks less than delighted and proprietorially takes hold of Georg's hand as she stands beside him.

One of the most well-known parables Jesus told was also about a return. The full story of the wayward younger brother who squandered his inheritance can be found in Luke 15:11-32. Unlike Maria, the prodigal son really did 'burn his bridges' when he left home. He insulted his family and squandered the money that he'd been given by his heartbroken father. He ended up literally living with the pigs, and Jesus' audience understood that was the ultimate indignity for any Jew. Yet in his desperation, physically, emotionally and spiritually, the young man came to his senses and realised he needed to return to his family and his father.

His older brother had stayed home, simmering with too much resentment to be happy to see his rebellious sibling. His reaction was so different from his father's, who loved his lost son, despite his actions.

We can only imagine the father's hurt as he yearned for his son's return. And although he would not have been singing 'My Favorite Things', he may well have sung through the Psalms, using those words of forgiveness and hope, lament and longing as he scanned the horizon day after day, year after year. Then one joyful day he spotted a distant figure walking slowly over the horizon, a sorry bundle of raggedy, dirty humanity, desperately hungry, deeply ashamed and fully expecting to be scorned by those he had once shunned. In an instant, his father forgot any vestige of dignity, picked up his robes and ran towards him; hair and cloak flying, arms outstretched in welcome:

> The father said to his slaves, 'Quickly, bring out a robe – the best one – and put it on him; put a ring on his finger and sandals on his feet. And get the fatted calf and kill it, and let us eat and celebrate; for this son of mine was dead and is alive again; he was lost and is found!' And they began to celebrate.
> (Luke 15:22-24)

Back at the von Trapp Villa, Maria has been absent while she sought God's will. She's no prodigal, but she did leave without due notice or a proper goodbye. Such is the love of the children and, as we soon see, the love of their father, that they welcome her home without question.

That is a heartening image as we are all assured of an unconditional welcome when we return into God's outstretched arms. Whenever, whoever, however and whatever we may have done to distance ourselves from Him.

Moments for musing

If you can, look at a copy of Rembrandt's painting 'Return of the Prodigal'.[13] What might it suggest to you about the characters, emotions and messages in this parable?

Where might you place yourself in this parable of the prodigal son, his older brother and his loving father?

If you are experiencing the sorrow of a 'prodigal' in your life, how are you praying, hoping and watching out for them?

Prayer

Dear Lord, You are the God of prodigals, so help me recognise if and when I wander too far and need to return into Your welcome embrace. Amen.

---

[13] www.rembrandtpaintings.com/the-return-of-the-prodigal-son.jsp (accessed 20 December 2022).

40
When the Lord Closes a Door...

After dinner, on her first night back at the villa, Maria wanders round the garden as the captain watches her from the balcony. The baroness joins him and attempts to distract her fiancé with suggestions of luxurious wedding gifts she could get him. Elsa knows that things are not right between them. She has already recognised Maria and the captain are in love, even if they have not acknowledged it themselves. Mid-conversation, there's a subtle change of pace as she and the captain tacitly reach a dignified understanding. Their wedding cannot go ahead. It's a carefully scripted dialogue indicating their mutual care and respect. Elsa suggests that out in the garden is a young lady who won't ever become a nun. With that prompt, she leaves Georg and goes and packs her suitcase.

The captain takes his chance and goes to the garden to find Maria, who is sitting by the gazebo. Their conversation is delightfully ambiguous, each of them in love yet ignorant of the fact that the other feels the same. It takes a while for the penny to drop... Then Georg tells Maria that Elsa is leaving, because he couldn't possibly marry someone when he is in love with someone else.

Maria's response is to melt into his arms in a blissfully romantic moment, murmuring how Reverend Mother had always said that when the Lord closes a door, He opens a window.

If you have ever searched for a new home to buy or rent, you will know the challenge of finding the right property at the right time. Over the years, as we searched for our next home (rather more often than we might have expected!), somehow things always worked out. After every initial disappointment, when we lost a potential house or couldn't sell our own property in time, we discovered retrospectively how each move had taken us further on in our journey of faith, so that we were ready for the next step.

Or perhaps you have had job interviews and were disappointed when someone else got the role you really wanted? But that rejection meant you were free to apply for a later opportunity more suited to you?

These are just two examples of the 'window opening after a door closes' principle that Maria is referring to.

Sometimes circumstances unfold in ways that don't appear to make sense. Yet in everything, good or bad, we can look back to see how nothing is ever a wasted experience. But looking positively forward into the unknown takes trust; and trust does not imply being so passive that we sit until an opportunity lands in our lap. Trusting while moving forward and exploring the way ahead means being willing to take steps to discern and explore. If we need biblical encouragement to understand that, then this verse is perfect:

> Trust in the LORD with all your heart,
> and do not rely on your own insight.
> In all your ways acknowledge him,
> and he will make straight your paths.
> (Proverbs 3:5-6)

After returning to the captain, I reckon Maria had not expected her dreams to unfold so quickly. Yet it is just as well none of us can see what's around the corner, for it isn't always what we might want to see. Of course, various occult practices seem to promise us a view into our future, but this is not of God.[14] Someone well versed in such things explained to me some years ago that fortune-telling can be based in one of two kinds of deceit: the human kind, where the 'fortune teller' manipulates a conversation through suggestion and guesswork, making spurious presumptive 'predictions'; and the other kind, exploiting darker forces and introducing occult powers into people's lives. Neither approach is godly or good; one is simple fraud, the other dabbles with evil spirituality.

Maria was experiencing how God will 'make straight' our path. That took an active faith where she, like us, needed to use her God-given intelligence, experience and emotions, while also trusting that He would unfold things in the right way at the right time. It was now clear that a new window of opportunity was opening as the abbey doors were closing. She was finding a way to use her love outside the convent to bring life and love to the whole von Trapp family.

---

[14] Read for example, Acts 16:16-18.

Moments for musing

Waiting for things to unfold can be so hard. What happens if you are stuck between one 'closed door' and a 'window' that's not yet opened?

How might we fully trust and 'not rely on [our] own insight'– while also fully engaging our God-given intellect and emotions?

Meditate on Proverbs 3:5-6. How might you acknowledge God in all your ways?

Prayer

Dear Lord, help me to trust You with all my heart and not rely on my own insight, and acknowledge You in all my ways and trust that You will make my paths straight. Amen.

41
Something Good

I have been itching to write about this song since starting Maria's story in *The Sound of Musings*. The captain has declared his love for Maria and so, in inevitable musical tradition, a song becomes essential for this romantic scene. And while the melody is charming, the lyrics always bothered me. How could a nun, even a soon-to-be-ex-nun, a woman of faith, suggest that what is happening to her now is the direct result of the good she did years ago? She sings that it must be the result of something half-decent she did, in her otherwise dejected past.

What kind of God is she referring to who only gives good things to those who do good things? That idea makes me very uncomfortable, for it reflects the spurious theology that God 'rewards' or 'punishes' us depending on our behaviour. And that is contrary to the whole concept of His unconditional love.

When I was a vicar, I'd sometimes hear people suggest to me that the tough times they were going through must surely be a punishment from God. Their understanding of God as a vengeful dictator who would wreak havoc in anger was so different from my own understanding and experience, and I would try to reassure them. Rather than send any punishment or wreak any havoc, God was with them in their troubles and ready to give His strength, comfort and help. His love and presence was assured, no matter what they may or may not have done in the past.

Bad things happen to good people, and people do suffer all kinds of things through no direct fault of their own. I know, for I gave birth to a baby boy many years ago who died when he was three days old because of a congenital heart defect. His little heart wasn't compatible with life even though the surgeons tried to fix it. That was no consequence of my, or anyone else's, bad decisions or sin. He didn't 'deserve' his life to be cut so short, and we as a family didn't 'deserve' the pain and grief it brought. I was simply the mum who had the 'one in 10,000' baby born with a life-threatening heart condition.

Anyway, who is perfectly behaved all the time? And how could we ever decide who deserves to be rewarded or punished by what they've done? Everyone does a range of both good and bad things in life. John wrote, 'If we say that we have no sin, we deceive ourselves, and the truth is not in us' (1 John 1:8). But the good news is, there is Good News!

> For while we were still weak, at the right time Christ died for the ungodly. Indeed, rarely will anyone die for a righteous person – though perhaps for a good person someone might actually dare to die. But God proves his love for us in that while we still were sinners Christ died for us.
> (Romans 5:6-8)

So perhaps we ought to listen to Maria's song again. She sings another line to Georg, who is standing in front of her and declaring his love for her; for whether he should or not, he definitely loves her. That declaration offers more evidence of God's grace and love. The incredible thought that despite our past, God reaches out to all of us, and stands by us, loving us, even though we may not deserve it. God's unconditional love and grace completely refute the idea that we get what we deserve! The joy that Maria and Georg discover is not a 'reward' for any 'goodness' on their parts but the consequence of seeking and trusting God. Maria has prayerfully sought God's will, so it shouldn't be a total surprise to discover such a blessing.

So that said, why, I wonder, do we find answered prayers such a surprise sometimes?! I remember, when buying our current house, praying with some lovely Christian friends that God would work out His purposes in our next move. Our house had been on the market for less than twenty-four hours when we received a surprisingly good offer to buy it. A sale that quick was not the norm in our area at that time. We started to pontificate; should we accept the offer…? Surely it was too quick…? Until our friends reminded us that we *had* prayed for guidance and help! Events then unfolded so miraculously that we could see God's hand on every stage of that house move.

There is, though, a real difference between a blessing and a reward. Blessings are not rewards, or good things that happen because we've been good, but the natural and supernatural outcomes of our good God who made our world a 'good' place, as we read in Genesis 1.

And now I've written about this song, I recognise there's another way of interpreting it. I appear to have focused so much on the one line that irritated me, that I missed the treasure of the next line. For Maria also sings of her incredulity at being loved by someone who seemed unavailable. So from this simple romantic song, we can remember two things: first, not to allow one irritation to blind us to a hidden treasure; and second, that God is always nearby, loving us.

Moments for musing

When did you first notice God was working in your life, perhaps before you knew Him?

We can all get annoyed about one aspect of an issue or one aspect of a person and fail to see the bigger picture. How might we keep an open mind to consider the whole picture?

How might reflecting on God standing before us, and loving us, *despite* all that we have done, influence our faith?

Prayer
Dear Lord, when bad things happen, help me turn to You for strength and hope and not indulge in self-pity. Amen.

42
The Bride

Maria and Georg now know what we've known for a while: that they are in love and meant to be together. So it is little surprise that the next scene opens with the sound of wedding bells ringing over Salzburg. We enter the abbey, to see Maria calm and composed in her shimmering, white wedding gown. She is poised and ready, any vestige of 'flibbertigibbet' long gone. She kneels before Reverend Mother to receive God's blessing; they both now know this is the right path for her to take.

The transformation of Maria is almost complete. Remember that first scene when she seemed young and awkward, running over the hills clothed in the simplest of dresses? Now she's about to marry her beloved captain, with his seven children; the very family that had engendered consternation not so long before.

In her familiar abbey, Maria prepares to leave one life and start another. She walks across the familiar courtyard and through large gates, which open into a cathedral-sized church where the marriage will take place. Watching her are her former 'sisters of the cloth', while before her are three of the von Trapp girls, Liesl, Marta and Gretl, dressed as bridesmaids. I always wondered why the other girls weren't bridesmaids too?

Then, with measured, graceful steps, Maria and her soon-to-be stepdaughters begin their (very) long walk up the aisle past the large congregation. She seems to glide towards her waiting fiancé, her dress and veil trailing like the wake of a ship. Taking the captain's outstretched hand, they ascend the steps to the high altar and kneel before the officiating bishop.

There's quite a lot of imagery in the Bible about weddings, images that reflect the relational aspects of God and His worldwide Church, drawn together in love and committing to an eternal relationship. In the book of Revelation, there's a hint of what is to come, a wonderful image of a great wedding supper, the 'marriage of the Lamb', when the 'bride', which is the embodiment of the Church, becomes as one with the Bridegroom, who is Jesus Christ. Yet unlike most weddings where the guest list is limited, the image of the Wedding Feast of the Lamb in Revelation is the one wedding we are all invited to:

> Then I heard what seemed to be the voice of a great multitude, like the sound of many waters and like the sound of mighty thunder-peals, crying out,
> 'Hallelujah!
> For the Lord our God
> the Almighty reigns.
> Let us rejoice and exult
> and give him the glory,
> for the marriage of the Lamb has come,
> and his bride has made herself ready;
> to her it has been granted to be clothed

with fine linen, bright and pure' –
for the fine linen is the righteous deeds of the saints.
(Revelation 19:6-8)

That will be the day when every divine promise of God will be fulfilled. Like a lot in the book of Revelation, this image of a bride meeting her Bridegroom draws on evocative images familiar throughout Scripture. Isaiah also used that wedding image to describe the joyful reunion between God and His people:

I will greatly rejoice in the LORD,
my whole being shall exult in my God;
for he has clothed me with the garments of
    salvation,
he has covered me with the robe of righteousness,
as a bridegroom decks himself with a garland,
and as a bride adorns herself with her jewels.
(Isaiah 61:10)

It is worth noting that the image of the bride, representing God's people, isn't gender-related, because churches are made up of all people, not just female brides. Sadly, though, we have to acknowledge that throughout history the earthly bride of Christ, the Church, hasn't always been so righteous. There has been a lot to repent of in so many ways. But there is the promise of redemption for all who seek it. For as Maria was transformed from gawky to graceful, the worldwide body of Christ, the Church, will be also be transformed by grace, and adorned in the shining righteousness of Jesus.

Meanwhile, until that day we can remember that for better or worse, richer or poorer, in sickness and health, our God is with us. And, unlike the covenant that brides and grooms make in a church wedding service which is 'till death us do part',[15] the covenant God makes with us lasts beyond human death, to life everlasting.

Moments for musing

How do those pictures of God's completed, redeemed kingdom affect how you think and act today?

Do you need to find support for any way the Church has failed you, or caused pain? Who will you ask for help?

What part do you play in your church, and how might you help it to grow and flourish?

Prayer

Dear Lord, help me live each day as if You are coming back tomorrow, keeping an eternal perspective. Amen.

43
A Shrewd Plan

In the month that Maria and Georg have been on their honeymoon, much has changed in Austria. Those abbey bells which rang so joyfully for their wedding now toll sombrely as the next scene opens. Ranks of soldiers are marching across the Residenzplatz in the centre of Salzburg and huge Nazi banners bedeck the buildings. A car with Third Reich flags fluttering screeches to a halt in front of the Felsenreitschule, which is a large theatre hewn out of rock standing in the centre of the city. Herr Zeller gets out and marches inside, where Max and the von Trapp children are rehearsing for the Folk Festival due to take place that evening.

We met Herr Zeller before, at the von Trapp grand and glorious party, when he and Georg were barely able to contain their mutual hostility. Now he announces himself as the newly appointed 'Gauleiter', a high-ranking paramilitary Nazi official appointed by Hitler to oversee the city. Herr Zeller demands to know when the captain will return from honeymoon and tells Max to pass on the message that when he does return, the captain will be expected to take his 'proper position' in the new order. Gretl watches him stomp off before asking Max why Herr

191

Zeller is so angry, and is it anything to do with the flags with the black spider on them?

Back at the von Trapp villa, the newlyweds have returned unexpectedly, a day early. Things have certainly changed there, too, for there's a Nazi banner hanging over the front door. It was hung by Herr Zeller and his comrades, but Georg rips it down in disgust and tears it up as Max and the children also arrive home. There is, as expected, joy and hugs as the family are reunited and the children call Maria 'Mother' for the first time. In their excitement, the children blurt out that they are going to sing at the festival that evening. The captain is quietly furious with Max: his children will not sing in public; no argument!

Liesl hands her father a telegram that Rolf gave her earlier. It brings news of his worst fears. He is ordered to report to the German navy the next day. With grim resignation he tells Maria that while refusing would be fatal, he could not even think about accepting the commission. They have no choice, and the captain and Maria decide together to leave Austria that night. Their plans are deliberate, secret and strategic, and while for the greater good, they carry great risk.

As followers of Christ, Christians are often required to make strategic plans, and recognise that some situations are complex and require great wisdom and tenacity. Jesus reflected that strategic planning when He sent the disciples out on their first mission: 'See, I am sending you out like sheep into the midst of wolves; so be wise as serpents and innocent as doves' (Matthew 10:16).

A thousand years before that, King David had given God thanks and praise after escaping from his enemies and the embittered King Saul. A situation not dissimilar to the captain and Maria's experience when escaping the Nazi regime. David was able to see how God had been with him:

> With the loyal you show yourself loyal;
> with the blameless you show yourself blameless;
> with the pure you show yourself pure,
> and with the crooked you show yourself perverse.
> (2 Samuel 22:26-27)

The von Trapp family need to escape, and by the grace of God they are given the opportunity to do so. They use their shrewdness to make plans, while wisely discerning the risks. To those who support them, like Max and the nuns, this is a brave and daring plan, while to those who oppose them, like Herr Zeller, this is, to quote King David, a 'perverse' escape.

When Jesus told His disciples to be as 'wise as serpents and innocent as doves', it implied we will need a canny combination of attributes. One way we could look at that is to flourish while not bringing undue harm to those around us. In some translations of that Bible verse (such as the NIV), the word used for 'wise' is 'shrewd'. But for a godly person, rather than being wily, shrewdness suggests using wisdom and a clear-headed practicality to make the best of a challenging situation.

Whatever situation we face, especially those that require tact, courage and integrity, we can trust the Holy Spirit to show us the way forward. Sometimes His means and methods might appear strange, but no one ever suggested that following God is boring!

Moments for musing

What kinds of situations, in business or work, church or home, need the dual approaches of wisdom and gentleness?

What kinds of leadership examples around you, or in the media, mirror that strategic approach?

How can you keep yourself positively shrewd without becoming 'wily'?

Prayer

Dear Lord, when I am in a tricky situation,
please help me to be as wise as a serpent and
innocent as a dove. Amen.

44
The Sun Always Comes Out

Between the newlyweds' arrival and their secret plans to escape, there is a little scene and song between Maria and Liesl worth looking at. Liesl has just called Maria 'Mother' for the first time, which she says sounds so nice. Maria replies she too likes hearing it.

Liesl then looks downhearted, and asks Maria what to do when someone you love stops loving you? We surmise it is Rolf, the telegram boy, who has broken her heart. Liesl has a problem and she has trusted Maria to be a safe person to whom she can go for advice. It would be too easy for Maria to dismiss this as misplaced teenage infatuation, but she responds sensitively. She says that when coping with unrequited love, you cry a little and wait, and one day the sun will come out again, for it always does.

Listening to this dialogue reminds me of a biblical principle that we who have been consoled and comforted by God have something worthwhile to pass on to others:

> Blessed be the God and Father of our Lord Jesus Christ, the Father of mercies and the God of all consolation, who consoles us in all our affliction, so that we may be able to console those who are in any

affliction with the consolation with which we ourselves are consoled by God.

(2 Corinthians 1:3-4)

Liesl recognises that Maria has found true love, even if it has not been straightforward. Therefore, she has experience to offer advice into her situation. It is important that we find the right people to seek advice from, those who have the character, sensitivity and experience to safely share our quandary.

Liesl admits there are many things she should know, but doesn't. Maria assures her that with age will come experience and wisdom; meanwhile, she understands what Liesl is struggling with. For sometimes, Maria confesses, she too has felt as if the world was coming to an end. They sing a reprieve of the earlier song, 'Sixteen Going on Seventeen', that Liesl sang with Rolf. What happened with Rolf was in the past, but the remnants of that previous song help to shape a new song of hope, beyond Liesl's lost love.

We need to experience a situation before we can understand it. When my baby son died, it was another bereaved mother who was the only one who *really* understood the depth of grief I felt. She had both the theory and experience to walk with me in my sadness. She understood enough of my sadness to be truly supportive, but she couldn't understand *exactly* how I felt, because she was not me and we all respond differently, even if our experiences are very similar. Ever since then I am so careful never to say to anyone, 'I *know* just how you feel.' Because I don't. I may have an *inkling* how they *might* be feeling, but I am not them. I do remember my friend saying that 'the sun will shine again', and although at the time that didn't feel possible, she was so right. I hung on to her experience that I would survive my own grief.

The only one who really does know how we feel is God Himself, as Psalm 139 explains:

> O LORD, you have searched me and known me.
> You know when I sit down and when I rise up;
> you discern my thoughts from far away.
> You search out my path and my lying down,
> and are acquainted with all my ways.
> Even before a word is on my tongue,
> O LORD, you know it completely.
> You hem me in, behind and before,
> and lay your hand upon me.
> Such knowledge is too wonderful for me;
> it is so high that I cannot attain it.
> (Psalm 139:1-6)

It is because God *does* know us that He is able to give us the strength and comfort we need, when we need it. Sometimes that will be in a supernatural peace and strength, or sometimes it will be by surrounding us with caring, supportive friends. Most of the time I have found it to be a mixture of both – God's strength and people's practical presence.

Then strengthened by Him, we can, at the appropriate time, effectively support others. And so grows a mutual support network with people willing to walk with us, whatever life throws at us.

I'd like to think that when Liesl was older, she became sensitive and wise enough for others to turn to. Pity there was no sequel to *The Sound of Music*. Yet!

Moments for musing

How have you been most comforted by others, by God?

What support can you offer others based on your own experiences?

When are good times to listen and not give advice?

Prayer

Dear Lord, thank You that You are the 'God of all consolation'. Help me to console others with the consolation I have received from You.

Amen.

45
A Change of Plan

To avoid his call to serve in the German navy, Georg and Maria have hatched a plan to escape from Austria with the children. That night, before the festival begins, the family, along with Max, take advantage of the darkness to push their car out of the garage and make a judicious exit. They fail to spot Franz watching them from behind an upstairs curtain; sadly, he has switched loyalties from being their faithful butler, and betrays them to Herr Zeller.

The family are dressed warmly, as Maria and the girls walk behind Max, Georg and his son Kurt, who are pushing the huge car, silently steered by his other son, Friedrich. Its engine is off because they cannot risk alerting anyone to their escape. Once outside the villa's gates and on the road, they breathe a sigh of relief and make ready to start the car and drive across the hills. However, in a flash, literally everything changes. They are caught in the glaring headlights of several official cars lurking to catch the family.

Herr Zeller steps forward and asks politely if they have trouble with their car. Both he and Georg feign innocence, even though both know exactly what's really happening. In a trice, Georg offers a plausible answer to say they are on their way to sing at the festival. We note the fleeting look of surprise on Max's face as he hears this; the family's dramatic change of strategy means he will get his new singing group on stage after all.

Maria picks up the 'festival' narrative and pleads with the soldiers to allow them to move on quickly, for the night air will affect the children's singing voices. Herr Zeller instructs his men to help the captain with his troublesome car, which, of course, starts immediately. Georg gives an offhand shrug and the family climb aboard, somehow all hiding their relief; they appear to have evaded imminent capture.

Most of us make plans, from whatever is on today's domestic to-do list to planning a distant holiday or big birthday bash. I remember being twenty years old and planning to have kids at certain ages (two boys and two girls) and expecting what I can only describe as a 'cornflake ad' family life... Not sure if that was arrogance or naïvety. It did not work out quite like that.

By nature, I am still a planner. I like to have things in the diary and to think ahead. However, by faith, I have learned that even when thwarted by an unexpectedly huge spanner in the works, it will yet work out all right, somehow. My security isn't in the plans themselves, but in God, who can be trusted if things unfold differently.

The Covid-19 pandemic showed how carefully mapped-out plans are actually so fragile. Everyday life changed quickly as postponed weddings and holidays, home-schooling and online working became the new norm. People had to accept new and distressing ways to manage illness and bereavement. It was definitely not easy, and for some it was heartbreaking.

Plans change because people change. Plans change because external circumstances change. But plans will never change because God might change; as the enigmatic writer to the Hebrews tells us:

> So we can say with confidence,
>> 'The Lord is my helper;
>> I will not be afraid.
>> What can anyone do to me?'
> … Jesus Christ is the same yesterday and today and for ever.
> (Hebrews 13:6,8)

God *is the same* yesterday, today and forever and holds both the beginning and the end of all things, giving us the ultimate framework for security and stability. There are few guarantees in life, but we can trust He is dependable, no matter what unfolds.

Two thousand years ago, the disciples discovered how an unexpected turn of events drastically affected their plans. I'm guessing they anticipated a long and fruitful life with Jesus, 'job security' for the next few decades. Jesus' mission would probably include overthrowing their Roman occupiers, and possibly those obdurate Jewish leaders too.

Except the disciples were looking through the wrong end of the telescope. Their vision was too small and blinkered. Their understanding of who Jesus really was and what He came to do was diminished by their human perspective. That first Easter weekend they hid in fear and despair after the crucifixion, all their plans, hopes and dreams shattered.

Yet early on Sunday morning the disciples began to hear stories that Jesus was alive; some women had seen Him, and Peter and John ran to find an empty tomb… Slowly the truth dawned and hope grew that what He had been telling them before might actually be true.

God's plan had not been thwarted; it had been fulfilled, perfectly. The cross was not an unexpected spanner in the works, but the means for God to achieve His ultimate plan. Jesus hadn't needed decades to convince people who He was; just long enough to do what was necessary. He took an eternity plus thirty-three years of humanity, plus three days at Calvary.

I have heard people say that to make God laugh all you have to do is tell Him your plans… That, I suggest, is a rather skewed representation of God's character. First, because we don't need to 'tell' God anything, as if He doesn't already know. And second, it conjures up a capricious, rancorous kind of God that neither evidence nor experience supports. God loves it when we share our inner hopes and dreams with Him, and so invite His Holy Spirit to work with us. I certainly don't believe that God ever maliciously scuppers plans, but He is perfectly capable of helping us adapt and cope with whatever happens, as Maria and Georg discover.

Moments for musing

Where in the Bible can you read how God guided and supported people's plans? Can you find some of His more unusual methods for guiding people?

Looking back on your life, when were your carefully drawn plans changed unexpectedly?

What can you learn about holding lightly to human plans and holding fast to God's plans?

Prayer
Dear Lord, help me trust You in the
uncertainty of life and be adaptable as I serve
and trust You. Amen.

46
Gone!

The tensions are rising as Maria, Georg and the children perform together at the Felsenreitschule, with its vast backdrop of stone alcoves. And just as Max predicted, they delight the audience. Considering it is such a last-minute addition to the programme, they do really well to produce such perfect harmonies and choreography!

Their joyful rendition of 'Do-Re-Mi' is in direct contrast to the stern faces of Herr Zeller and his comrades. They are waiting to escort Georg to his enforced naval command after the festival, with soldiers stationed around the auditorium in case he plans to escape. The looming threats are all too evident.

Georg steps into the spotlight to introduce the next song. It is a love song for his country and he picks up his guitar to sing 'Edelweiss'. His voice falters with emotion, so Maria joins him, followed by the children. Then the audience join in the singing too, as Herr Zeller and his cronies watch stony-faced.

At the end of the song, the auditorium erupts with applause and Max takes the stage to declare the conclusion of the festival. He tells the waiting audience that while the judges deliberate their scores, the von Trapp family will sing an encore. He explains how this will be their last song together before Captain von Trapp takes up his command in the Third Reich.

Perhaps it's that dichotomy between the charming singing alongside the threat of the military presence that makes this so poignant? One by one, the children sing their verses of 'So Long, Farewell' and scurry into the wings, leaving Maria and Georg to sing their last goodbyes before they too leave the stage. With those last notes echoing over the empty stage, Max steps forward to announce the competition results. Third place goes to... (Slow down, Max, please speak slower, I urge.) Second place goes to... (Go on, Max, just keep that funny lady bowing a few more times to give the family more time to escape...) Then at last, all too quickly, Max announces that the winner and the highest honour in Austria goes to... the von Trapp Family Singers...

Trumpets fanfare and applause rings out over an empty spotlight on the vacant stage. Max tries again and announces the winner a second time, 'The von Trapp Family Singers...' There is a tense moment, an awkward pause, before a lone soldier runs in shouting that they have gone. However often I watch this movie, my heart is in my mouth each time!

This scene reminds us of that other, 'He's gone!'

'He's gone,' whispered the terrified Roman guards (see Matthew 28:11-15).

'He is not here; for he has been raised,' assured the angelic messenger who greeted the women (Matthew 28:6; see also Mark 16:6; Luke 24:5).

The Gospel accounts tell in no uncertain terms that Jesus was crucified; He was dead and buried. Yet despite every attempt to keep Him buried, He vanished from under the very noses of the soldiers appointed to guard the tomb. The Roman and Jewish authorities who had wanted Jesus killed were determined to ensure there was no way His corpse could be removed to propagate absurd claims that Jesus had come back to life. For once, those usually embattled authorities had worked together, no chances taken. Yet despite their efforts, His very dead body vanished from the tomb, and soon His followers were telling everyone that Jesus was really alive. Surely too ridiculous to believe?

Yet, He had really come back to life, although a new and different dimension of life. We read how after His resurrection, Jesus could enter a room despite a locked door (John 20:26) and could vanish at will (Luke 24:31). He was able to eat and drink, be touched and be very present with those who knew Him (Luke 24:36-43). He was very much alive, yet had a new kind of body – a resurrection body. It is the kind of body that we too are promised, by faith:

> But in fact Christ has been raised from the dead, the first fruits of those who have died. For since death came through a human being, the resurrection of the dead has also come through a human being; for as all die in Adam, so all will be made alive in Christ. But each in his own order: Christ the first fruits, then at his coming those who belong to Christ.
>
> (1 Corinthians 15:20-23)

Two thousand years ago, they knew what 'dead' looked like, and there had definitely been a dead body in the tomb when the stone rolled it closed that Friday:

> When the sabbath was over, Mary Magdalene, and Mary the mother of James, and Salome bought spices, so that they might go and anoint him. And very early on the first day of the week, when the sun had risen, they went to the tomb. They had been saying to one another, 'Who will roll away the stone for us from the entrance to the tomb?' When they looked up, they saw that the stone, which was very large, had already been rolled back. As they entered the tomb, they saw a young man, dressed in a white robe, sitting on the right side; and they were alarmed. But he said to them, 'Do not be alarmed; you are looking for Jesus of Nazareth, who was crucified. He has been raised; he is not here. Look, there is the place they laid him. But go, tell his disciples and Peter that he is going ahead of you to Galilee; there you will see him, just as he told you.' (Mark 16:1-7)

The women expected His body to be where they had left Him hastily as the Sabbath dusk began on Friday evening. Yet on that first day of the new week, as the sun was rising, they saw the Son Himself had risen. And because actions speak louder than words, we see now why He had refused to be drawn into power struggles or human arguments with cynical detractors. He had not needed to prove Himself or justify who He was, because His actions and the evidence would speak for themselves.

God in human flesh lived among us, born of a woman, the long-expected Messiah. Every divine, ancient, scriptural promise was completely and utterly true. Jesus had conquered death, despite His very real human demise, because, quite simply, you cannot kill God. If Jesus didn't rise from the dead, then the Christian faith has no basis at all (see 1 Corinthians 15:12-20). Yet He did rise from the dead, as the angels announced... and the disciples discovered, 'He's not here, He's gone! He's been raised!'

Back in Salzburg, there is no point looking for Georg, Maria and the von Trapp children in the Felsenreitschule, because they have gone; which is an uncomfortable truth for those tasked with securing Georg's conscription – pretty much like those Roman soldiers when their dead prisoner disappeared. Although, we could have some sympathy, for it wasn't actually their fault; no human guard could keep Jesus buried in that tomb.

Normally that kind of escape from under the noses of hostile guards would signify the end of the story. Although for the von Trapp family, as it was for Jesus' followers, it was anything but the end...

Moments for musing

What do you personally think and feel about the resurrection?

What evidence can you think about of changed lives after the resurrection?

What does it mean to say Jesus has 'conquered death', or 'death has lost its sting' (see 1 Corinthians 15:54-57)?

Prayer

Dear Lord, help me live with the truth of the resurrection embedded in my heart. Amen.

47
A Safe Haven

Georg, Maria and the children have slipped past the soldiers at the festival and made their escape. It is literally life or death now as their plan unfolds. The captain has shown that he's very much against Hitler's cause, so if they are caught, then he and probably the whole family will be punished, very severely.

Fortunately, those of us who have seen the end of the film can rest assured. Although you, like me, may still feel that frisson of excitement each time the family hide within the catacombs.

Where would you run if your life were in danger? For Maria, it is evident she knows their sanctuary is with the nuns at the convent, with the people of God, her family. And, as Maria hoped, Reverend Mother doesn't hesitate, and hides them without obvious consideration for her own safety.

So many brave people offered sanctuary and hiding places to those escaping Nazi persecution. Stories like those of Corrie Ten Boom,[16] or Anne Frank[17] are just two among so many of people who both hid and were hidden, despite the danger they faced.

Thousands of men and women like Reverend Mother overtly or covertly challenged the harsh regime. Yet, despite their bravery, it is still utterly shocking how so many people were swept up into such an evil ideology that inflicted malice and murder upon fellow human beings. We humans too often fail to learn from the horrors of history. Yet, in the face of such ongoing horror, people continue to stand up for righteousness and justice, or speak out for those who have no voice.

Persecution of innocent people is not new or limited to one culture, creed or time. The slaughter of early Christian believers under despotic Roman emperors like Caligula and Nero shaped the early Church. Jesus warned His disciples that they were going out like 'lambs into the midst of wolves' (Luke 10:3). He warned too that, 'Those who find their life will lose it, and those who lose their life for my sake will find it' (Matthew 10:39). The cost of following Jesus in some cultures can be colossal, however eternally magnificent the glory might be.

Today, millions of Christians face threats and severe repercussions for declaring faith in Jesus Christ. It becomes a daily challenge to stay true to their faith, and they do so with great bravery and determination. We cannot imagine such a constant and visceral threat. Living

---

[16] Corrie Ten Boom, with John and Elizabeth Sherrill, *The Hiding Place* (London: Hodder & Stoughton, 2004).

[17] Anne Frank, *The Diary of a Young Girl* (London: Penguin Classics, 2019).

in a democratic country means we can meet openly to worship God without fear of arrest or danger. Although, some suggest, there are many subtle ways the Christian faith is growingly undermined today in the UK.

Our own safety from such imminent danger does not give us any excuse to ignore the perils our brothers and sisters in Christ face daily. One organisation working with the persecuted Church, Open Doors, tells that even today, hundreds of millions of Christians face high or extreme levels of persecution for their faith.[18] We, who live in freedom and democracy, can give support by standing with them in prayer and action.

Even when declaring faith in Jesus does not pose a life-threatening risk, it can cause rifts in families and challenge all kinds of personal and business situations. And for those converting from other religions, it can be a hugely sacrificial decision. Even in safe cultures, it can be very daunting to admit we believe in Jesus Christ and our beliefs may incur cynicism, apathy, incredulity or derision. We may fear being labelled weird, or judgemental and out of step with today's society. We may fear being caught out by a theological or biblical question we cannot answer; yet, in many countries, that is the least of their concerns.

Reverend Mother took a massive risk when she locked the gates to the catacombs so that Maria and the family could hide in the darkness. For us, the greatest risk is to *unlock* the boldness and compassion of God to face our own reservations and fear, and share our faith freely and openly.

---

[18] See www.opendoorsuk.org (accessed 20 December 2022).

Moments for musing

What do you know about the persecuted Church? How might you discover more and perhaps become actively supportive?

How secretly do you live out your faith?

What could you do to show and share the love of God to those around you, in a way that is both compassionate and appropriate?

Prayer
Dear Lord, we pray for those who face persecution today for Your sake. We pray for their strength and safety, and that those who oppress them will discover Your transforming love. Amen.

48
I Lift Up My Eyes

Maria and Georg have escaped with the children and are seeking shelter in the abbey. Just behind them their pursuers close in, and it is going to take a miracle to keep them safe. But then, God's really good at what we might call miracles; to Him they are part of what He does, a normal, everyday divine act.

Reverend Mother leads the family to the catacombs behind the abbey; it's a place full of tombs, gravestones and hidden corners. Not the sort of place most people would run to under normal circumstances, but then Reverend Mother isn't 'most people'. Set along the back wall are larger tombs behind locked gates. She opens the wrought-iron gates so the family can find a place to hide in the shadows. Then, after locking them, she gives Maria the key. She has already told Georg and Maria there can be no escape by road because the army has closed the borders. The only way to freedom will be on foot, over the hills. The situation is desperate, yet she reminds Maria they are not alone, for God will be with them. Then she quotes from Psalm 121: 'I will lift up mine eyes unto the hills, from whence cometh my help' (KJV).

The language and imagery of Psalm 121 would be especially evocative for those living amid the Austrian mountains in Salzburg, although it was originally sung by pilgrims on their way up to Jerusalem. It is a song asking for protection and declaring trust. The words are a dialogue, asking and answering questions:

> I lift up my eyes to the hills –
> from where will my help come?
> My help comes from the LORD,
> who made heaven and earth.
> He will not let your foot be moved;
> he who keeps you will not slumber.
> He who keeps Israel
> will neither slumber nor sleep.
> The LORD is your keeper;
> the LORD is your shade at your right hand.
> The sun shall not strike you by day,
> nor the moon by night.
> The LORD will keep you from all evil;
> he will keep your life.
> The LORD will keep
> your going out and your coming in
> from this time on and for evermore.
> (Psalm 121)

The first line is somewhat enigmatic and could be either a question or a statement. Are the hills the place of safety, or are they a place of danger where perils and menace lie in wait? Whichever the interpretation, the answer is in the next verse... wherever we go, the Maker of those hills is our defender and guide.

We are realistic; we know that no journey is guaranteed to be safe; incidents happen when we least expect them. This psalm isn't promising absolute *safety* through life's journeys; it is promising *security*. This is a song of trust for all who 'pilgrim', who travel through the sometimes hilly and rocky places of life and need reassurance that they are not alone.

It is appropriate that this scene is set in a cemetery, for our ultimate journey will be from life through death and into whatever lies beyond. Our final journey will probably be the greatest challenge we face, but it need not hold a crippling fear of the unknown, for on that journey too, God is with us.

For hundreds of years, St Peter's cemetery in Salzburg has been the final resting place for thousands of life's pilgrims, and is an open cemetery still. It is a real place in the heart of the city, and inspired the setting of these catacombs in the film.

As a vicar, you get used to cemeteries and graveyards. But being 'used to it' doesn't mean there are easy answers in the midst of real suffering and grieving. Yet there is always hope and security in the Lord, who 'will keep your going out and your coming in from this time on and for evermore' (Psalm 121:8).

His divine promises are for everyone and, like the iron key Reverend Mother gave to Maria, faith and trust is our 'key' to security and freedom. The iron key that locked them in was the same key that unlocked the gates, and as the family then escape to freedom – oh no… I've just given the ending away!

Moments for musing

What is the difference between seeking safety and seeking security?

What do you think about your last journey, leaving life here to go beyond your last breath? How might this psalm inspire you?

What helps you feel secure?

Prayer

Dear Lord, as I journey through life, thank You that You never 'slumber nor sleep' and always keep watch over me. Amen.

49
I'm Scared

Maria, Georg and the children are hiding while soldiers search for the fugitive family. In the darkness, Marta whispers that she is scared. She is not alone, for Brigitta admits it too.

As they crouch in the shadows, Gretl asks Maria if now would be a good time to sing about their favourite things? She's got the right idea, but Maria whispers this is one time singing would not help. She urges her to keep very quiet and gathers Gretl into her arms as they try to make themselves disappear into the darkness.

The soldiers are getting closer and rattle the wrought-iron gates behind which the family are hiding. Those gates might offer a locked barrier, but no safety, for a bullet would go straight through them. As the soldier's torch beam plays around them, they huddle further out of sight, hardly daring to breathe…

We can scarcely imagine how terrifying it would have been for this family, hiding from such mortal danger; yet many people live with fear and in fear. That whispered confession 'I'm scared' is not limited to young children, and not limited to critically perilous situations. All of us feel scared at times.

I admit to feeling scared of things that aren't actually dangerous, like big spiders. My head assures me they are safe, but my heart disagrees. Yet if it were a poisonous spider, like the white-tailed spider I encountered up close and personally in Australia a few years ago, then I would have reason to feel fear. White-tails look innocuous, but I was warned their bites can cause a very nasty reaction.

For something to be really justifiably scary, then it needs to not only pose *imminent* danger but be *close enough* to actually do so. To be both present and potent. A poisonous spider behind glass cannot cause any harm even if I watch it from an inch away, because although it's present, it's not actually potent through the glass. It's close, but not close enough to be a real danger.

So when I am afraid, I need to ask if I am really facing danger. A snake on television might make my toes curl, but it can't do me any actual harm. The grass snake that slithered across my path just in front of me on a recent walk was very present but not potent.

Fear is a natural and God-given response to keep us safe. Having no fear would be highly ill-advised if we became reckless and put ourselves or others in danger. So we need fear, but in its proper place. And we need to recognise when we have become fearful of something that doesn't actually pose the danger we are anticipating.

Even Jesus had to face His very real fear, for fear is a legitimate response to imminent danger or pain, and all of us will experience legitimate fear at times. Jesus was fully human and not immune to the pain and fear that lay ahead when facing His crucifixion. He knew what was about to happen to Him. We read Luke's account of Jesus' anguish at Gethsemane. Luke was a doctor and the one Gospel writer to include the detail that Jesus was sweating 'drops of blood'. Even today, sweating blood is a rare phenomenon, but still a verified medical condition called hematidrosis and is caused by extreme stress:

> He came out and went, as was his custom, to the Mount of Olives; and the disciples followed him. When he reached the place, he said to them, 'Pray that you may not come into the time of trial.' Then he withdrew from them about a stone's throw, knelt down, and prayed, 'Father, if you are willing, remove this cup from me; yet, not my will but yours be done.' Then an angel from heaven appeared to him and gave him strength. In his anguish he prayed more earnestly, and his sweat became like great drops of blood falling down on the ground. (Luke 22:39-44)

I have never considered myself particularly brave. I spent years avoiding situations and experiences like fairground rides or being up somewhere high, and getting very worked up when faced with dentists. I labelled myself 'a wimp' for ducking out of things, until I learned a lesson about what being brave actually is.

We were on a stopover in Singapore having visited family in New Zealand. My husband and then eight-year-old son wanted to take the *very* high cable car over to visit Sentosa, an island in the bay. Did I tell you it was very, very, extremely, horrendously, ridiculously high? Way beyond my comfort zone. So it took a huge (*huge*) amount of persuading to even think about going on it. But in the end, with trembling legs and pounding heart, I set aside my abject fear to give my son the experience he begged for.

With my eyes firmly shut, we dangled hundreds of feet above the harbour, swishing and swinging along the cable in our *glass-bottomed* four-seat gondola. I sang a worship song very loudly and very out of tune, trying to generate some confidence during those fifteen long minutes that felt like fifteen hours.

I was terrified, but I did it. I did it because my love for my son was greater than the fear of the present and potent danger I saw in that cable car. I began to recognise that doing something despite being terrified is actually brave, not wimpy. I had mistakenly thought brave people weren't frightened or worried about something; that somehow they bypassed the emotion of fear. They don't.

You don't need to be a superhero to be brave; bravery is facing something despite the nerves. Being brave is going to seek medical help when something feels wrong, especially if it might be serious. Being brave is facing up to a bully, or challenging someone who is treating another person badly. Being brave is standing up for what is right, even if those around you keep quiet. Being brave is stepping outside your comfort zone, for the right reasons.

My youngest son is called Joshua. His name is inspired by the Old Testament hero who was tasked to lead God's people across the River Jordan into the Promised Land. It was the final stage of the Exodus begun by Moses decades earlier. Over and over, God told Joshua to be 'strong and courageous' (Joshua 1:6-9). The task would not be easy, and it would be fraught with physical danger. Yet Joshua was not alone, for God was with him:

> As I was with Moses, so I will be with you; I will not fail you or forsake you. Be strong and courageous;

for you shall put this people in possession of the land that I swore to their ancestors to give them. Only be strong and very courageous, being careful to act in accordance with all the law that my servant Moses commanded you; do not turn from it to the right hand or to the left, so that you may be successful wherever you go ... I hereby command you: Be strong and courageous; do not be frightened or dismayed, for the LORD your God is with you wherever you go.

(Joshua 1:5-7,9)

My own Joshua is now an adult and a firefighter, with his namesake's urging to be 'strong and courageous'. Firefighters are not immune from fear when they run into burning buildings, or arrive at a serious incident with unknown dangers lurking. But my son, and so many others, do it despite their trepidations. Bravery is not being reckless or ignorant; it is understanding the seriousness of a situation and still facing it, for the greater good.

Jesus went to His cross despite His real fear of the pain and horror ahead. Yet His love for us was greater than His fear, for only through the cross could He rescue us from our own fears. And because of Gethsemane and Calvary, we have the promise of a Saviour who not only understands our fears, but also offers a way through what is probably our greatest human fear – the fear of death.

As they crouch in hiding, Maria hugs Gretl close. Together they face a very real danger with understandable human fear. Yet in their fear, the image of Maria holding the child offers us a lovely image of how God holds us when we are afraid. When we are that close to God, we can almost hear His whispered assurances that it is 'in his arms' that we can take refuge (Isaiah 40:11), until all fear has ceased.

Moments for musing

What situations evoke fear when danger isn't actually 'present and potent'?

How are you brave?

When faced with a scary situation, which Bible verses might be helpful to you personally to face those fears?

Prayer

Dear Lord, in the face of real or perceived
threats, help me be brave and courageous and
remember that You are with me always.
Amen.

50
I Have Sinned

The family have evaded capture by the soldiers and escape to the hills using the abbey's car, where they will continue their journey on foot to Switzerland. Realising the family have slipped past them, the soldiers leap into their cars to give chase. Yet for some reason their cars will not start. Time and time again their engines hiccough and rumble, but they fail to get the cars moving.

Inside the abbey, Reverend Mother watches, while Sister Margaretta and Sister Berthe stand behind her looking penitent. She turns to them as they confess that they have sinned. As the abbess asks what they have done, the guilty pair reach under their voluminous habits to bring out two parts of an engine. Those canny nuns had the understanding and skill to remove what look like the distributor and an ignition coil, without which the cars cannot function.

I think the wry smile on Reverend Mother's face echoes my own opinion of that unnecessary 'confession'! I believe God champions those who are oppressed and persecuted and gives the understanding and skill to do what is necessary to assist them. There was no real 'sin' to confess.

In my experience of church, we can talk about sin so much that sometimes it seems the sole purpose for meeting together! We could start to think we are naught but wretched sinners, grovelling, waiting to be humbled before a stern, judgemental God.

Yet 'sin' is real, even if it is an unfashionable word. Sometimes we may use the word 'trespass' or 'debt', but these words all relate to the same principle of marring God's image in us – those times we think, speak and act in ungodly ways; those times we trespass into places that we should not go… Sin hurts our own selves and negatively affects those around us. And we all sin, because we are fallible and human. The only person who never sinned was Jesus. He never broke any moral or holy law. His humanity was real enough, yet because His divinity was real too, He had both the *free will to choose how to live* and the *holiness to choose not* to sin.

God cannot sin, will not sin, nor tempt others to sin. Sin is as incompatible with God's nature as dinosaurs were to catching a train! Yet when we inevitably get things wrong, the Holy Spirit prompts us to accept responsibility and put things right. Not because God is grumpy and enjoys telling us off, but because He wants us to become the very best we can be.

So God made a way to reconcile us to Himself through our Saviour, Jesus. The holy, sinless One became the broken One on the cross; not because of anything we deserve, but because of His grace and love. That is why Jesus' agony was so intense, because *all* the world's sins were piled on top of His physical agony. It must have crucified His soul as well as His body; no wonder Jesus cried out, 'My God, my God, why have you forsaken me?'

(Mark 15:34). In that moment, for the first time He experienced total separation from God's love because of the weight of sin, and it was excruciating. He paid the outstanding debts for all humanity for all time, on our behalf, setting us free from debt forever. Our balance sheet of sins, trespasses and debts is eternally cleared. When we *accept* His gift of forgiveness, we become transformed by faith and take on a whole new identity, the nature of Jesus, no longer seen by God as 'sinners', but as His adopted, redeemed, holy children. Paul describes this transformation and calls us 'saints':

> So if anyone is in Christ, there is a new creation: everything old has passed away; see, everything has become new! All this is from God, who reconciled us to himself through Christ, and has given us the ministry of reconciliation.
> (2 Corinthians 5:17-18)

And yes, we are all works in progress; even saints (and nuns!) need to say sorry at times! Yet a sinning 'saint' isn't relegated to the status of 'sinner' again. We may be saints who sin, but our core identity is assured, despite our tendency to fail and fall away at times.

We know that Maria and the family escaped to freedom and lived to sing again. Theirs was a physical escape to inhabit a new land with the freedom and opportunity that gave them. When we put our faith in Christ, we find freedom from the burden of sin, and are invited to embrace our complete new identity as a forgiven child of God.

Moments for musing

What is your real, inner identity?

How might you embrace the freedom that Jesus offers?

How does it feel to be loved by God for who you are, not what you do?

If you haven't ever intentionally placed your life into God's hands and accepted His gift of eternal forgiveness, could today be the day that you take that step? This prayer may help you start your new adventure of faith to walk in the freedom of God's unconditional love:

Prayer

Dear Lord, I willingly accept Your gift of forgiveness for all that I have done that has dishonoured Your image in me. Help me embrace the truth that by faith in Jesus, I really am a new creation, a saint, and secure in Your love and grace forever. Amen.

51
The Walk to Freedom

The Sound of Music is a long film and ends as the captain leads his family across the hills. He is carrying Gretl on his back as the children and Maria follow behind. The scenery is stunning, reflecting the film's opening scenes with those glorious views of Maria's mountains. This whole drama has been wrapped in the promise and glory of God's creation. Yet while the views in both the overture and the finale may look similar, so much has changed in the characters.

The captain is no longer distant, austere and severe. The children have rediscovered their love for life and music, and Maria is no longer a disorganised, naïve, novice nun. She has become a wise and loving wife and stepmother, has captured the hearts of Georg and his children, and has discovered the life she was born to live.

I like that image of Georg carrying Gretl; presumably it has been a long walk and her little legs can't carry her any more. That image reminds me that when I feel unable to keep going, God has and will metaphorically carry me too.

The family follow their father, trusting that the path he takes them on will be the best path. Their climb is fraught with danger and exhausting, but the prize of freedom and safety will be worth every ache along the way. Of course, it is a film; yet we may be equally familiar with similar trials and treks. Burst blisters, hunger and thirst and the inevitable question, 'Are we nearly there yet?' However... with eyes fixed on their goal, the family reach safety to escape persecution and Georg's military call-up.

I remember my first taste of such a climb, on a school field trip in the Derbyshire Peak District. It seemed fitting that our circular clamber meant leaving and returning to the little town of Hope, for it was the concept of 'hope' that kept me going up hill and down dale.

We know God never promised us an easy life, but He does promise to walk with us, no matter what:

> Do not fear, for I have redeemed you;
> I have called you by name, you are mine.
> When you pass through the waters, I will be with
>   you;
> and through the rivers, they shall not overwhelm
>   you.
> (Isaiah 43:1-2)

The von Trapp family walk to freedom across the hills, as the music soars and the credits roll. There then follows a very long list of each person involved with the film's production; so many deserving a name check! Not just the actors, but all whose particular skill made this film possible. Like many memorable projects, it takes a lot of people to get a film from first draft to final showing...

Which makes me wonder: looking back, who will be on my list of rolling credits at the end of my life story? Like a film, there will be some major players, while others take smaller if significant parts. I wonder if they know how important they have been? It's mind blowing to think how many lives we all contribute to, hopefully positively! Like great movies, lives are not solitary events, or solitary productions. We are all part of a great interconnected adventure, with many watching and investing in us.

Like Maria, we are all offered the chance to discover and fulfil God's will for our life. When we decide to appoint God as our 'producer' and the Holy Spirit as our 'director' and Jesus as our 'leading protagonist', then whatever story plays out, the metaphorical film of our life will have an eternal impact for the glory of God.

May you too discover the life you were born to live...

Moments for musing

Who do you credit as significant in your life, and what difference have they made?

We have walked with Maria through the film to discover what God's will for her life is. What might God's will be for this time in your life?

What are the most significant things you will take away from this film – and this book?

Prayer

Dear Lord, help me remember You are my 'producer', 'director' and 'leading man'. Help me trust that You will always stay close, even carry me, right to the 'end credits' of my life and beyond, into eternity. Amen.

52
A Good Story

'Once upon a time…'

Once upon a time, there was a beautiful princess who kissed a frog who turned into a handsome prince…

Once upon a time, deep in the heart of Sherwood Forest, a bunch of outlaws led by Robin Hood stole money from the rich to give to the poor…

Once upon a time, there was a nun who was a governess to a lonely widower and his seven children. She stopped being a nun and married the widower, and the family became famous for their singing.

'Once upon a time…' Stories enrich our lives, inspire, entertain, soothe and challenge us. Stories weave a narrative around events and relationships that capture our attention and connect with our emotions. Whether based on facts or fairy stories, myths or legends, people have shared stories as long as humans could talk. It's an aspect of the image of God we inhabit; the ability to share ideas, be creative, recount events, entertain and educate.

Stories tend to follow a pattern; they need characters and a setting. They need a plot; literally a 'story' to take us from opening scene to conclusion. Often, but not always, they end 'happily ever after'. Along the way, there will inevitably be some kind of conflict, when something or someone forces the characters to tackle a problem. The outcome of that struggle drives the story to its conclusion.

When she was six, my granddaughter proudly explained a proper story shape she'd learned at school: Introduction; Climax/Catastrophe; Rising Action; Falling Action; Resolution. I was so gobsmacked at her literary understanding that she wrote it down for me to remember. I didn't know the meaning of such words when I was six, much less have any concept of a story's shape. Now when I read any story, including God's 'story', I can recognise elements of that shape.

Good storytelling is a compelling art and something Jesus perfected, for He was the master storyteller. His parables were beautifully crafted, and set within a common cultural context. Jesus used stories – parables – to comfort those who were challenged, and challenge those who were too 'comfortable', or complacent.

One day after listening to the parable of the sower (Luke 8:4-8), Jesus' disciples asked why He used parables. He answered:

> To you it has been given to know the secrets of the kingdom of God; but to others I speak in parables, so that
> 'looking they may not perceive,
> and listening they may not understand.'
> (Luke 8:10)

The parables were not designed to confuse or exclude, but to challenge His listeners. He wanted them to respond to God's open invitation, but that needed faith and an open heart. Jesus understood it was hard for people to believe, or to recognise *who* was in front of their eyes. Now, as then, it needs a spiritual revelation to recognise and accept God's truth. Easy messages and easy lessons can be too easily forgotten. We usually need to grapple with something to truly understand and remember it. The parables had that extra depth to prompt a listener to really think, to grapple with the message that revealed God's love.

Like every good story, the Bible has compelling characters, intriguing plots, twists and turns, war and peace. It starts at the very beginning(!) in the garden paradise (Genesis 1,2) where God dwelt with His people in mutual love. And ends, many thousands of years later, when God and His people will dwell eternally in mutual love and relationship. This time living in a renewed heaven and earth, where the River of Life flows through the New Jerusalem (Revelation 22:1). This is one book where we're encouraged to peek at the final chapter; for rather than it spoiling the ending, it will encourage and inspire us to trust as we wait.

Back on earth, once upon a time a real nun called Maria Augusta Kutschera was born in January 1905, married Captain von Trapp and later died in March 1987.[19] She was a postulant at Nonnburg Abbey in Salzburg and I remember, as a child, watching her on the BBC children's programme *Blue Peter*. She was a real person, and had written a book that inspired *The Sound of Music*, albeit a fictionalised Hollywood interpretation of their actual story. It became, as we now know, one of the most popular

---

[19] www.archives.gov/publications/prologue/2005/winter/von-trapps-html (accessed 28th February 2023).

films of the last century. It won five Academy Awards including Best Picture in 1965 and offers us an example of 'faction', which is fiction based on facts.

When we turn to the Bible, it's also helpful to consider what genre of 'story' we are reading. Rather than just one book, the Bible is sixty-six different books, of many different literary genres. Together they make up the inspired word of God, offering divinely inspired poetry (like Psalms), prophecy (like the Old Testament prophets), letters (like Paul's letter to the Ephesians or Galatians) and historical accounts (like Joshua, the Gospels or the Book of Acts). It is awe inspiring how these ancient writings still offer something new and relevant each time we read them, no matter how familiar we become with any passage. That's because the Bible is not just printed text, but the words of God which point us to the Living Word of God, Jesus, as Paul explained:

> All scripture is inspired by God and is useful for teaching, for reproof, for correction, and for training in righteousness, so that everyone who belongs to God may be proficient, equipped for every good work.
>
> (2 Timothy 3:16-17)

Those seeking God's truth have read it throughout the centuries and found it as applicable and inspiring as we do today. How incredible that the Bible has proved so real, relevant and life-giving across every generation, community and culture.

And in one way we could say it's incomplete, for there are simply too many more stories of God's promises, provision, power and love to fit into any single text. Yet what we are given is more than enough to draw us into a relationship with God, to show us what is important. We read what He deems sufficient and pertinent for us to understand His character and purposes. The disciple and Gospel writer John acknowledged the challenge of trying to summarise all Jesus did:

> This is the disciple who is testifying to these things and has written them, and we know that his testimony is true. But there are also many other things that Jesus did; if every one of them were written down, I suppose that the world itself could not contain the books that would be written.
> (John 21:24-25)

What we have, in the Bible, is just an introduction, a foreword, a taster to draw us in. Words that invite us to grapple and discover His glorious truths. Words to help us discover His love and purposes. Words to articulate God's eternal love story to draw us in and recognise our rightful place in it. For while there are millions of books offering self-help and inspirational materials, for the real truth that changes lives for all eternity, we need look no further than the Bible.

Moments for musing

What do you believe about the accuracy and reliability of the Bible?

What is 'your story' and how does that interact with God's story?

How might you (re)read The Bible with the added understanding of it being God's inspired, personal word to you?

Prayer

Dear Lord, thank You for your persistence in sharing Your love; thank You that I am free to read Your inspired Word. Help me recognise Your truth and take my place in Your unfolding eternal story. Amen.

Sound of Musings Live!

Contact Bryony to invite her to your church and host a themed missional event with a difference.

It's going to be inspiring, honest, faith-filled and quite a lot of fun... An event you can invite members and 'not yet' members of your church to be encouraged as we journey with Maria as she discovers more about life, love and faith.

Author Bryony Wood will be sharing from her life and her book about the hidden joys in this iconic film and living in God's love.

You might even offer 'tea with jam and bread' and 'crisp apple strudel' and an impromptu singalong...

To contact Bryony or to invite her to speak at your church, email: bryony@bryonywood.co.uk
website: www.bryonywood.co.uk

Study guide

Download *The Sound of Musings* Study Guide from Bryony's website, www.bryonywood.co.uk. It's a FREE resource for churches who would like to run a six-week small group inspired by this book, and is accessible and biblically based. It is aimed at both those in church already and those 'just wondering'.

It would be great to know how you get on if you use it – contact Bryony through her website or social media #bryonywoodwrites

Acknowledgements

Like any good film, there are a lot of people to thank, so these are my 'rolling credits' at the end of the show.

The Sound of Music was an inspiration for my own faith journey, so a good starting point upon which to muse all things faith-filled. I just needed a prompt to stop dreaming and start writing. And that was given by Rt Rev Martyn Snow, my then bishop. Until then, I'd kept *The Sound of Music* as my 'guilty secret' for a rainy Sunday afternoon. But he was the first man I knew who divulged he liked the film too, and yes I should write about it. Turned out, he and I are not the only *Sound of Music* aficionados in the world. The more I spoke about this idea, the more voices gathered in a chorus of approval, indicating this might be worth writing. So thank you, Martyn. I really appreciated your initial and subsequent encouragement.

So, at the very beginning, this offered a welcome distraction in the Covid-19 lockdown. I would watch the film scene by scene with notebook in hand, constantly surprised by every little prompt of the Holy Spirit as each message and musing became clear. I never imagined we'd find more than fifty musings from just one film.

Thank you to Rev Frances Finn at BBC Nottingham, who spotted the potential of *The Sound of Musings* as a mini-radio series on her Sunday morning show – that was fun! And Andrew Halloway, the editor of *Good News* newspaper,[20] who commissioned 'Sound of Musings' as a monthly column. Both of you gave me a wider platform and confidence that this was worth sharing.

The next two who were instrumental in this evolving from blog to book were Debbie and Chris at Core Publications Ltd. You both were so generous and supportive with your time and expertise. I am so grateful; you understood me and this project, and helped me believe I could offer this to a publisher. Which leads me to Instant Apostle. You are such a kind, professional bunch of people and I feel truly blessed to work with you. You're an answer to prayer. Thank you especially Nicki Copeland and Sheila Jacobs for seeing through my initial waffle and recognising the value in this, and your encouragement along the way. We share the passion to produce more accessible resources, so more people will find it easier to share the love of Jesus. Thank you!

Thank you also to Emma Wood for your sensitive and quite miraculous photography and author photos.

To those named at the start of the book who read proof copies and offered reviews, I am truly grateful and somewhat humbled. To a first-time author your endorsements mean such a lot, and I know you squeezed reading my draft book into already overfull diaries, so thank you for making the time to read and comment.

Lastly, to all my patient and encouraging friends, including Jane Pearce, Jenny Moxon, Maggie Scott,

[20] www.goodnews-paper.org.uk (accessed 10th January 2023).

Christine Kent and Rod Hinton, who read drafts and who all asked how it was going – thank you!

Bryony